DUQUESNE STUDIES

Theological Series

2

God's World In The Making

DUQUESNE STUDIES

Theological Series

2

God's World In The Making

by

PETER SCHOONENBERG, S.J.

DUQUESNE UNIVERSITY PRESS

Pittsburgh, Pa.

EDITIONS E. NAUWELAERTS, LOUVAIN

1964

DUQUESNE STUDIES

THEOLOGICAL SERIES

Henry J. Koren, C.S.Sp., S.T.D., Leonard A. Bushinski, C.S.Sp., M.A., S.T.L., S.S.L., Leonard J. Swidler, Ph.D., S.T.L., editors.

Volume One—*Albert Dondeyne*, FAITH AND THE WORLD. XI and 324 pages. Price: $5.00 cloth.

Volume Two—*Peter Schoonenberg, S.J.*, GOD'S WORLD IN THE MAKING. IX and 207 pages. Price: $3.95 cloth.

In preparation:

William H. van de Pol, *Anglicanism in Ecumenical Perspective.*

Henry Fries, *Bultmann—Barth and Catholic Theology.*

Imprimatur

Dr. A. van Kol, S.J. a.h.d.
Trajecti ad Mosam
die 12 Aug., 1963

Library of Congress Catalog Card Number 64—12599

Printed in the U.S.A. by
The AD PRESS, LTD., New York, N.Y.

ii

DUQUESNE STUDIES are published in the following series:

African Series

Philological Series

Philosophical Series

Psychological Series

Spiritan Series

Theological Series

Catalog on request. There is a twenty percent discount on continuation orders for any series.

PERIODICAL PUBLICATIONS of Duquesne University Press:

Annuale Mediaevale ($4.00 per year)

Duquesne Hispanic Review ($3.00 per year)

Duquesne Review. A Journal of the Social Sciences ($2.25 per year)

Duquesne Science Counselor ($3.00 per year, $3.25 outside U. S.)

Journal of Ecumenical Studies ($6.00 per year, $6.50 outside U. S.)

Review of Existential Psychology and Psychiatry ($5.00 per year)

CONTENTS

PREFACE

This book has grown from articles published by the author in various periodicals. In order that these articles might be suitable for incorporation into a single book, they have been integrated and harmoniously connected into chapters, in such a way that substantial repetitions do not occur. However, to make it possible for each chapter to be studied as a distinct unit, a few minor repetitions have been retained or introduced. By claiming that each chapter can be read as a distinct unit, I do not wish to convey the idea that the chapters are disconnected. On the contrary, my sole reason for uniting them into a single book is precisely the fact that each of them represents a single view of the topics discussed.

This view is expressed in the title, GOD'S WORLD IN THE MAKING. All chapters are concerned with the *world,* understood not simply as the physical universe in opposition to man, but as the world in which man himself is involved precisely insofar as man is not merely a part of nature. This world is viewed as *in the making* and developing; i.e., as participating in a process of evolution and a drama of human history. Finally, the title speaks of *God's* world, because the author constantly endeavors to see this world as God's creation, and as continuously growing toward the "fullness of Christ."

Each of the book's chapters is an encounter between human science and human reflection, on the one hand, and our faith in divine Revelation, on the other. As a theologian, the author bases himself primarily on God's Revelation. In other words, his encounter with human science and reflection takes place from the standpoint of theology and Christian philosophy.

In my explanations of Bible texts and doctrinal statements of the Church, I have always endeavored to distinguish their content, meaning, or message from the context of the world-view and the picture of man in which they were originally formulated. I considered myself justified in following this procedure for the reason that divine Revelation is not intended to impose a particular view of the world or a particular picture of man, but to be a message of God's love addressed to all men of all times.

For this reason also, it would not have been sufficient simply to divest the message of Revelation from the ancient world-view in which it is clothed. I am writing for my contemporaries and therefore wish to throw light on the meaning of this message for today, for the man who has our own modern view of the world and of man. This aim implies that I may not be satisfied with the simple statement that the static world-view of the biblical writers does not pertain to the revealed message itself. The object of my investigation is precisely to discover, in the light of God's self-revelation as a God of history and in the light of Christ as "the last Adam" (1 Cor. 15:45), what is the meaning of the temporality, the evolution, and the history which are the atmosphere in which we moderns experience our being-man.

The author plainly wishes to acknowledge the fact that his thinking has been influenced by his French fellow-Jesuit Pierre Teilhard de Chardin. The recognition of this dependence does not mean that I consider Teilhard de Chardin a kind of a new Saint Paul, a Thomas Aquinas, or a Saint John of the Cross. With Jean Guitton I see in him "more the prophet of a new vision than its master."[1] What I have written in this book likewise bears the character of the essay rather than that of a definitive formulation.

The above-mentioned words of Guitton are quoted twice with approval by Robert T. Francoeur in his introductory contribution to *The World of Teilhard de Chardin*.[2] I was agreeably surprised to find in him and in other contributors to this book an attitude of critical openness, and trust that this same attitude manifests itself in my own work.

---

[1] "Le phénomène Teilhard," *Informations catholiques internationales,* Vol. III (1960), pp. 28 f.
[2] *The World of Teilhard de Chardin,* ed. by Robert T. Francoeur, Baltimore, Helicon Press, 1961, "Introduction: A New World Vision," pp. 12 and 23.

Preface

I sincerely hope that the American edition of this book will contribute to the great encounter between Faith and evolutionary thinking which permeates our contemporary world. This edition has been made possible by Duquesne University, which invited me as a visiting professor to lecture for one semester on the topics treated in this book. Among those who have been particularly helpful to me, my special gratitude is due to Reverend Father Walter van de Putte, C.S.Sp., the translator.

Duquesne University   PETER SCHOONENBERG, S. J.
Easter, 1963

CHAPTER ONE

EVOLUTION

The vision of Teilhard de Chardin has stimulated Catholic thought in a new way. We can foresee that it, together with the biblical renewal, will provide materials for a new theological synthesis. Such a development is noticeable since the publication of Teilhard's works and the translation of some of them, especially *The Phenomenon of Man* and *The Divine Milieu*.[1] Moreover, we are faced with the whole ideology of evolutionism as well as with existential philosophy, and it is our primary task to give evidence of a *searching* faith, of a search to determine the content of faith in a dialogue with man's modern view of himself. One who searches in such a fashion does not fail to get results even now. He sometimes obtains a more profound experience of the greatness proper to the Creator and Father of our Lord Jesus Christ in a world that is both "anthropogenesis" and "Christogenesis." It is in this spirit that the following thoughts have been written down.

Someone has said: "Isn't the way of thinking pursued by Teilhard and his followers totally different from that of Scripture? The latter looks at things from the standpoint of their final fulfillment, whereas they think from the standpoint of beginnings." There is a certain amount of truth in that contrast. However, when we examine it more closely, we realize that the proposition is too simplistic. As Karl Rahner has explained, Scripture considers things from the standpoint of the salvific present as pointing to the future.[2] Of course, the

---

[1] Pierre Teilhard de Chardin *The Phenomenon of Man*, New York, 1961, Torchbook ed., 1962. We refer to the Torchbook edition. Pierre Teilhard de Chardin: *The Divine Milieu*, New York, 1960. Excellent essays on the ideas of Teilhard followed by a bibliography of English literature about him, are published in *The World of Teilhard de Chardin*, edited by Robert T. Franceur, Baltimore, 1960.

[2] Karl Rahner: "Theologische Prinzipien der Hermeneutik eschatologischer Aussagen," *Schriften zur Theologie*, IV, Einsiedeln, 1960, p. 401-428.

Bible—which in its first book, *Genesis,* describes various "origins"—does contain considerations of beginnings, but this is rather in line with Israel's own vision of the past, which likewise proceeded from the salvific present. An evolutionist thinker, on the contrary, starts principally from the past and examines it to the extent that it can be known by the study of fossils and other remains. Even in this case, however, an experience of the present is the background of his vision of the past and the future.

This reflection may help us to determine more exactly what the true difference is between the two standpoints. Teilhard's vision is an interpretation of experimental data. Occasionally, however, he is a "philosopher in spite of himself"[3] and even to some extent, likewise in spite of himself, a theologian. Scripture, on the other hand, begins with God's word and our faith. That is why there is no immediate possibility of integrating evolutionistic and scriptural thought. We must really be on our guard in this matter and take steps to avoid the tendency to indulge in a kind of "concordism." What we should do first is to look for some meeting ground on which Teilhard's "phenomenology of the universe" or "hyperphysics" can be confronted with faith. This meeting ground lies in *meta*physics or, speaking more broadly, in philosophy.

It is a long time since theology laid claim to the title of "queen of the sciences" and it certainly no longer pretends to have "direct dominion" over them. Theology expresses rather the atmosphere of salvation within which research and thought develop according to their own laws. Theologians realize better than formerly that they should not consider divine Revelation as a substitute for, or a complement to, that research and thought.

Neither does theology direct philosophy. It rather provides it with inspiration. On the other hand, philosophy receives inspiration also from the world view constructed by the sciences of nature and mind. That's why philosophy is the proper platform for the meeting of theology and science.

[3]P. B. Grenet, *Pierre Teilhard de Chardin ou le philosophe malgré lui,* Paris. 1960.

2

Thomistic philosophy is also increasingly aware of this fact, as is evidenced by recent publications.[4] Hence we shall deal with the problem primarily from the philosophical standpoint, confining ourselves to a few theological thoughts toward the end.

EVOLUTION AS A PHILOSOPHICAL CONCLUSION

"One generation passes and another comes; but the world forever stays."[5] These words of the Preacher already show clearly that the earth, to the mind of the writers of the Sacred Books, is not subject to change. The earth has its "eternal mountains";[6] before they were formed God alone was;[7] and their eternal existence is an image of God's fidelity.[8] The same can be said with even more reason about the firmament with its fixed cycles.[9] Against the background of that stability there are only the generations of men, and no doubt also those of other living beings, that come and go.

Is this evolution? Certainly not, for the generations following one another remain within the species; the kinds of plants and animals, and the species "man" also, were formed at the beginning in that way and forever, according to the description of God's work in the first chapter of Genesis.[10]

This is the description proper to Antiquity and it has dominated our thinking until and even in the eighteenth century.

---

[4]Compare, e.g., N. Luyten's article, "Evolutionisme en wijsbegeerte," *Tijdschr. voor Philos.,* Vol. 16 (1954), pp. 3-35, with Karl Rahner's "Die Hominisation als theologische Frage," Paul Overhage and Karl Rahner, *Das Problem der Hominisation. Ueber den biologischen Ursprung des Menschen,* Freiburg, 1961 (*Quaestiones disputatae* 12/13).

[5]Eccl. 1, 4. Scripture is quoted according to the Confraternity of Christian Doctrine's translation, ed. *St. Joseph's Bible,* Catholic Book Company, New York, 1962.

[6]Hab. 3, 6.

[7]Ps. 89, 2; Prov. 8, 25.

[8]Is. 54, 10.

[9]Jer. 33, 20-25.

[10]When Gen. 2, 7 and 3, 19 say that man was formed "of" the earth and Gen. 2, 21, 23 similarly speaks of the formation of the woman "from" the man, they indicate not so much a historical origin as a relationship: "you are dust." Karl Rahner expresses this clearly in regard to the formation of the woman (*Die Hominisation,* pp. 24 ff., footnote 6); he could have brought this out more clearly in like manner regarding the formation of man (*ibid.,* p. 24 ff.),

The ancient Greek philosophers Heraclitus of Ephesus and Anaximander of Miletus thought in terms of evolution, but they had no followers. There is systematization but no "history" in Aristotle's "Natural History." After Linneaus (1707-1778) had completed his classification of the "System of Nature," he continued nevertheless to adhere to the description of Genesis and proclaimed that "there are as many species as were created from the beginning."[11]

Nevertheless, Linneaus brought to completion centuries of study about living nature. They made it evident that there is unity and interconnection throughout nature and that there exists an order from the less to the more complex, from lower to higher forms of life. However, alongside this order "in space", another order, that of time, had still to be discovered. This discovery was made later: the lower and therefore earlier strata of the earth were found to contain either only the lower forms still existing today or more primitive forms, related to our present higher forms. This evidence is strongest with respect to vertebrate animals. Thus we find in chronological order fishes, amphibians, reptiles, mammals, and besides these, intermediary forms that are now extinct. We conclude from this that the higher forms evolved from the lower. To be "after" means to be "derived from." Evolution is a fact. This conclusion has been confirmed by further discoveries since Lamarck (1744-1829) and Darwin (1802-1889). The picture has been completed by hypotheses and we have thus been given an idea of the entire visible world as an evolving whole, of living beings springing from the non-living, of man evolving from the highest mammals, from "primates," as they are called in biology. Teilhard de Chardin especially has given us the most universal expression of that vision.[12]

---

[11]Linneaus himself repeatedly qualifies that expression, thus leaving room for the later development of variations. For a survey of his expressions see H. J. Lam, *Evolutie. Een poging tot synthese in algemeen begrijpelijke vorm*, Leiden, 1946, pp. 27 ff.

[12]Cf. B. Delfgaauw, *Teilhard de Chardin*, Baarn, 1961; *Geschiedenis en vooruitgang*, Part I, *Het ontstaan van de mens*, Baarn, 1961; *Het vraagstuk van het materialisme* (inaugural address), Baarn, 1961.

We see, then, that we accept evolution not because we have witnessed it as an event or have caused it to come about, but we reason on the basis of discoveries. Hence the theory of evolution, whether total or partial, is not the result of something we have observed or the fruit of an experiment; it is a conclusion. This conclusion, however, was reached spontaneously, for the observations themselves were guided by an intuition.

This, after all, is what always happens. If I have known someone rather well when he was a boy, I recognize him ten years later as a young man and another ten years later as a father of a family. I don't conclude that the boy, the youth, and the adult whom I knew at different times are three different persons. I know spontaneously that the boy developed into the present man, because I am intuitively certain that I now face the very same person. Conversely, I recognize in a portrait of a youth the grown up man who stands before me.

Scientists act in the same way when they conclude to the existence of a successive development of species from one another, although the unity they intuitively perceive here is not that of a person but of a phylum of living beings, of the kingdom of plants or animals, or of the whole visible world. The process of knowledge, however, is fundamentally identical, although the unity in question is much more complicated and there is therefore greater danger of error and a greater need of verification.

The truth of a conclusion that accepts the growth of an individual or the evolution of a phylum depends ultimately on the question of whether or not the intuition of unity that serves as its foundation is true. The validity of an all-embracing theory of evolution depends on the question whether the visible world is truly one or not.

Delfgaauw has given a clear expression of this dependence in the following words:

> The idea of evolution is nothing but the direct conclusion from the apprehension of the unity proper to per-

ceptible reality. But, in saying this, are we not shifting and evading the problem? For, what shows us that perceptible reality is one? Are we not equally justified in holding that perceptible reality is divided into a number of separate units or "spheres" having no connection of any kind among themselves? Could we not say that the three kingdoms of the lifeless, the living, and human beings are entirely separate and independent?

The following objections can be made to this opinion. First of all, we are here concerned with perceptible reality as such. There is, in principle, the unity that connects what is perceived with that which can possibly be perceived. That is why modern science is based on the postulate of the unity of perceptible reality. A postulate is not a proof, but it is a fundamental prerequisite for adopting a particular attitude of mind. If science were to reject the unity among the things that can be perceived, it would make itself impossible. Science, moreover, enlarges its possibilities to the extent that it sees a more extensive field as a unity.[13]

Delfgaauw reasons here on the plane of ontology which, as understood by him, is philosophy inasmuch as it directs its attention to visible reality precisely as *visible*.[14] Ontology in this sense is therefore distinct from metaphysics, for the latter has for its object reality as such, which embraces also invisible reality. Scholastic philosophy identifies itself particularly with the latter metaphysics, but it seems to me that it will merely confirm and render more profound the unity affirmed by Delfgaauw and the knowability which he postulates. When scholastic thought seizes the whole of reality as "being," it thereby affirms real agreement, union, interrelation and unity, unless it wishes to engage in purely nominalistic play. And this unity is not merely that of not-being-nothing, but it consists further in the inexpressible positivity that is being-in-itself, being-oneself, in short,—being.

When man discovers the summit, the core and foundation of all being, which we call God, that unity of all reality

---

[13]Delfgaauw, *Teilhard de Chardin*, pp. 96 f.
[14]Delfgaauw, *Geschiedenis en vooruitgang*, vol. 1, pp. 78-83.

becomes even more evident. The one Creator makes creation also to be one. The Transcendent is the immanent bond uniting all things. In Him we live and move and are, and on that account we exist with and in one another. These considerations may help to show that scholastic, and in particular Thomistic, philosophy serve to confirm the starting point of evolution. We might perhaps say that the acceptance of evolution is demanded precisely by what the Encyclical *Humani generis* calls "the philosophy that is accepted and recognized by the Church."

We say, "perhaps." For, it is still possible that we are too hasty when we translate the general unity of being into the evolutionary interconnection of the visible world. The unity of all that exists, no doubt, brings with it a special unity of visible beings, but must we say that the latter unity is such that those beings proceed *from* one another? Is it necessary to conceive that unity as one of *causal* relation? It is our opinion that these questions must be answered in the affirmative.

Every connection of the visible or the invisible world can be understood only as giving or receiving a share in being. This implies causality, or at least is accompanied by it. A mere likeness in structure without any communication and dependence is simply incomprehensible and puzzling to us. True, scholastic philosophy speaks about exemplary causality, but this causality is an abstraction and really a contradiction if it is understood as not imparting any being, for to this extent it is precisely not causality. That is why Platonic thought rightly includes a participation in being and a dependence in being, in its concept of the relation between exemplar and "exemplatum."

Applying all this to the visible world, it seems that there is also a possibility that the lower beings might be caused, as a kind of diminished product, by the higher. However, this possibility is acceptable only as long as we abstract from the factor of time. For, when we pay attention to the actual successive appearance of various beings in time, we notice

7

that, broadly speaking, the higher forms always appear after the lower. Their causal connection likewise does not appear as if the lower being is a diminished product of the higher, but the lower seems to evolve toward the higher. Thus, we realize that the higher proceeds *from* the lower. In this way, we are not only prompted to accept evolution because of the modern way of thinking and the modern experience of life, but, paying attention to the sequence in time, we are also led to accept evolution on the basis of traditional thinking.[15]

Up to this point, we have limited our considerations to the visible world. But scholastic theology could object on the basis of the invisible world. It could say: There are angels and their existence proves that there can be creatures that have no causal connection with our world. Since that situation is possible within the whole of creation, is it not possible to have creatures within the visible world that are not causally related to the other visible creatures?

To this we could reply, first of all, that theology has not said the last word about angels and that it has in fact not even said the first word.[16]

---

[15]This implies that we no longer accept "authorities" in every field of knowledge. It was done in the Middle Ages with the result that there was no interest in observation and experiment. We have renounced also the medieval concept of the world as cloistered within narrow boundaries of time and space. Cf. Romano Guardini, *The End of the Modern World*, New York, 1958, especially Chapter One.

[16]The *existence* of personal created spirits does not follow apodictically from the mere fact that Scripture mentions them in numerous places. This existence likewise is not absolutely guaranteed by the position they occupy in the liturgy and the doctrinal statements hitherto made by the Church. So far as Scripture is concerned, as Karl Rahner explains in his articles *Angelologie* and *Dämonologie* (*Lexikon für Theologie und Kirche*, 2nd. ed., Freiburg i. Br., vol. I, col. 533-538 and vol. III, col. 145-147), Scripture presupposes rather than affirms the existence of good and evil spirits. Regarding tradition, it is doubtful whether it adds anything in this matter to Scripture. With respect to liturgical feasts, historical changes of the calendar of Saints show that such feasts do not necessarily exclude the non-existence of their object. So far as doctrinal statements of the Church are concerned, for the Fourth Lateran Council (1215) the issue was not the existence and the creation of angels and devils, which the Albigensians themselves accepted. The crucial point, affirmed by the Council against the Albigensians, was that everything

Evolution

Moreover—and this brings us to the heart of the difficulty—we are not justified in conceiving created spirits as being entirely foreign to our visible world. Hence we should not maintain that only through God's external appointment they have any connection with our visible world. If we conceive their spiritual character in that "pure" manner, we abandon the vision of creation as a totality and go back to Leibnitz's ideas of "monads." We are then far removed from the way Scripture pictures them expressing their relation to our world, as when it gives them names such as messengers, dominions, powers, thrones. We believe that the created spirits, like all creatures of the same God, should not and even cannot be thought of otherwise than as belonging to the one creation and therefore as having a causal connection with our visible, evolving world. We do not mean by this that they are products of evolution, but that they nonetheless exercise an influence upon the world, whether we are naturally able to perceive this influence or not. The human person is built, and continues to build itself, on the basis of the world below him. Perhaps we can point to a contrary direction in regard to the world of the angels, and say that the angel attains

that exists has been created by one God (cf. Denziger, no. 428). In other words, even this doctrinal statement, which most explicitly speaks of angels and devils, presupposes but does not directly affirm their existence (Cf. A. Darlapp, *Dämon*, III, *Lexikon f. Theologie und Kirche*, vol. III, col. 142). For this reason, theologians should ask themselves whether they can claim without qualification that this existence is "de fide." One could object that the Encyclical *Humani Generis* contains a warning against the doubt "whether angels are personal creatures" (Denziger, no. 2318). The context, however, makes it clear that the denial is either an "error" or merely contains "a danger of error."

Theologians should further ask themselves whether the existence of angels is a presupposition required by the content of other revealed truths or merely pertains to the world-view that served as a context in which these truths were revealed. Note, however, that even if angels and devils belong to this context, this fact does not prove that they do *not* exist.

All this should teach us to view Revelation as a message of God's love for us and of salvation rather than as instructing us in the nature and kinds of beings existing in the whole of creation. What Revelation tells us, in connection with good and evil spirits, about the dangers of sin and about God's willingness to come to our aid is more important than our knowledge concerning these spirits themselves.

fullness, whatever the manner might be, by communicating himself to the visible world.

However, most opponents will not argue against evolution on account of the difficulty created by the existence of angels. They will rather find the greatest objection from the standpoint of God. They will ask whether the Creator himself has not been left out of the picture in the preceding considerations. After all, God can without any difficulty create something new. Why then assume that what is new in the visible world is produced by what went before? Since we intend to reply to this objection a little later from the standpoint of God's creative action, we will restrict ourselves here to the following remark: When God creates something new within this visible world, this new reality likewise is *in* that world, it belongs *to* that world. And we are thus brought back to the ideas we have expressed concerning the causal connection of creatures and are led once more to accept an origin from a pre-existing world.

Hence, while remaining on the philosophical plane, we feel obliged to conclude that, within the visible world, that which is new comes *from* what pre-exists, and what appears later arises from what went before. But it belongs to the natural sciences to determine more precisely what things went before and what things came later and thus establish the fact of an ascent from the lower to the higher in a particular case. Moreover, those sciences must also specify how that evolution came about.

Accordingly, the philosophical assertion is concerned with evolution only in a most general way. It positively opens our mind for the acceptance of the conclusions reached by the natural sciences. That is why we prefaced our considerations with that assertion. But let it be understood that this philosophical affirmation cannot impart greater certitude to any scientific affirmation than is given by the data and reasonings that constitute the foundation of those scientific conclusions.[17]

[17]At most, arguing on the basis of hylomorphism, one might have a preference for saying that prime matter is disposed by lower forms

Precisely because the conclusion drawn by philosophy is so general, it belongs also to the particular sciences themselves to determine the degree of certitude of their own scientific account of evolution. That is why we abstain from making a choice between the terms "hypothesis," "theory," and "doctrine" as applied to evolution. Theology has even greater reasons for abstaining from such declarations, since Revelation does not make any pronouncements regarding the arguments proposed within the limits of a particular science.

EVOLUTION AND THE ANALOGY OF BEING

We have seen that the very general affirmation of evolution within the visible world is based on the general unity of this world. In scholastic thought this unity of being is already given a more concrete form and spoken of as analogy.[18] There is analogy between God and creature and between the degrees of being within creation. If we unfold this analogy regarding the visible world still further, it can bring us even closer to evolution. It then shows us the steps of the evolutionary process but without the element of time and movement, more or less like a frozen fountain.

When we express our intuition of the whole of reality in the idea of "being," this idea not only embraces that in which all things agree, but also and equally that in which they differ. The idea of being does not abstract from the differences found in beings but includes them, for the differences also are real. The idea of being expresses therefore

---

before being informed by higher ones. Cf. St. Thomas, *De potentia,* q., 4, a. 3, *ad* 33; *De veritate,* q., 4, a. 3c, and *Contra Gentes,* bk. III, ch. 22: "The ultimate end of the whole process of generation is the human soul, and to it matter tends as toward its final form."

[18]In this sense Teilhard de Chardin is more on the side of those who hold the scholastic doctrine of the analogy of being than on that of the existentialists who oppose freedom to nature. August Brunner, S. J., levels a negative criticism against Teilhard from the latter standpoint in "Pierre Teilhard de Chardin: a Critique," *Theology Digest,* Vol. VIII, No. 3, 1960, p. 143. Léopold Malevez in "The Method of Teilhard and Phenomenology," p. 137, same No. of *Theology Digest,* contrasts Teilhard with the thought of phenomenological existentialism and at the same time points out the partial agreement of Teilhard's vision with the scholastic concept of being.

that beings at the *same time* agree with, and differ from, one another in their being, that they *totally* agree and *totally* differ. This mutual relation between beings is precisely what is called analogy. It signifies therefore a relation of both agreement and difference, and these two do not occur outside but within one another.[19] Hence the idea of being is affirmed analogously of man and animal, for men and animals are not only beings to the extent that they agree, but the rationality and personality by which man differs from the animal is also something that *is*.

Analogy, however, is not merely a relation between diverse ways in which the idea of being is affirmed of various realities. Analogy is also a relation of reality itself, since knowing consists precisely in being with reality and coinciding with it, for in man reality, being, is conscious of itself.

Analogy is *the* relation of beings with one another, and to the extent that all our concepts are attuned to reality, we also realize that we use them analogously. This is true not only with respect to the transcendental ideas expressing the properties of being itself, such as the ideas of unity, truth, and goodness. It is also true of the concepts that express certain categories, e.g., that of man, for he who correctly attunes his concept of man to reality realizes that he does not abstract from the differences existing among men, such as sex, nationality, culture, and individuality. These differences do not exist outside but within man. Analogy is *the* mutual relation within the unity of being.

Scholastic philosophy is interested especially in the analogy between God, the infinite Being, and creatures, the finite beings. But, in connection with the topic considered here, we should like to call attention to the analogy between finite beings, to the analogy that exists within the world, in comparison with which the analogy between God and creatures could be called an "analogy of the second power." Analogy

---

[19]A. van Leuwen, "L'analogie de l'être. Genèse et contenu du concept d'analogie," *Revue néoscol. de philos.* Vol. 38 (1936), pp. 293-320, pp. 469-496; John A. Peters, *Metaphysics. A Systematic Survey,* Pittsburgh, 1963, Nos. 54-56.

manifests itself within the visible world principally between three degrees of reality: the lifeless, living beings below man (we need not examine the relation between plant and animal for our present purpose), and man.

We often consider whatever is below man and in contrast with man as a person, to be "things," objects, at the disposal of the person and over which the person has dominion and control. This view is correct. It is even a biblical and Christian view (cf. Gen. 1:26-29). But this opposition is not the only view, for within the opposition and the difference itself there is also agreement.

Physical science, on the other hand, prefers to begin with material reality and to study its composition ever more thoroughly. It is inclined to look upon life, and certainly upon consciousness, as something superadded, as an epiphenomenon.

The first view and tendency may be called spiritualistic, the second materialistic, without at once making these terms serve to express an evaluation. When Teilhard tries to synthesize those two views, he in fact merely concretizes the metaphysical analogy existing within the world by using it on his "hyperphysical" level. He maintains that the relation existing between man's spiritual soul and his body (or rather his materiality) has its analogous counterpart in the world of living things and the lifeless. This point must be developed further.

Contemplating the cosmos, Teilhard too begins with unity and reaches analogy. He finds agreement in every aspect, but within it he sees also differences according to the degree in which the agreement is realized:

> An irregularity in nature is only the sharp exacerbation, universalized to the point of perceptible disclosure, of a property of things diffused throughout the universe, in a state which eludes our recognition of its presence. Properly observed, even if only in one aspect, a phenomenon necessarily has an omnipresent value and roots by reason of the fundamental unity of the world. Whither

does this rule lead us if we apply it to the instance of human "self-knowledge"?

"Consciousness is only completely recognisable in man", we are tempted to say, "therefore it is an isolated instance of no interest to science." "There is evidence for the appearance of consciousness in man," we must continue, correcting ourselves, "therefore, half-seen in this one flash of light, it has a cosmic extension, and as such is surrounded by an aura of indefinite spatial and temporal extensions."

The conclusion is pregnant with consequences, and yet I cannot see how, by sound analogy with all the rest of science, we can escape from it. It is impossible to deny that, deep within ourselves, an "interior" appears at the heart of beings, as it were seen through a rent. This is enough to insure that, in one degree or another, this "interior" should obtrude itself as existing everywhere in nature from all time. Since the stuff of the universe has an inner aspect at one point of itself, there is necessarily a *double aspect to its structure,* that is to say, in every region of space and time—in the same way, for instance, as it is granular—*coextensive with their Without, there is a Within to things.*[20]

Hence the lifeless, which Teilhard prefers to call the "pre-life," has a "Within" which is analogous to human consciousness and also to the consciousness of living beings below man. That is why Teilhard speaks of the "conscious particles" of matter and occasionally even of "free particles." Now consciousness and freedom are the two modes of activity by which man realizes himself as a person. It seems to us that to the extent that we obtain a clearer view of this connection we also see somewhat better the analogy with lifeless matter.

Man is a person. It is true we have been taken into and situated in the world. We were procreated by our parents, are organically sustained by plants, animals, and oxygen. We are subject to the laws of heredity and are placed in a network of social relations. Constructive and destructive

[20]*The Phenomenon of Man,* p. 56.

14

processes are at work in our organism, and our death will be caused by some influence from within or without, an influence to which we are subject.

At the same time, however, every man stands in the midst of all that, as an "I," as a person, who is not the product of a sum of influences but takes those powers in hand to change them or give them meaning. Hence the person increasingly makes the body *his* body and the world *his* world. Every person stands like a fixed point amidst the waves of influences and remains himself; he *is*. But this is more than the stability of a rock amidst the floods, for the person has knowledge of it; he is himself and knows that he is.

Man is in-himself and so grasps himself, is transparent to himself. In other words, a person is conscious. Consciousness is being conscious; it is a manner of being, not something superadded to it in an accidental way. A person doesn't merely *have* consciousness; he *is* consciousness. Being-in-itself attains such a depth and greatness in a person that it is also a knowingly-being-with-itself, a consciousness. Personal being is therefore a being-in-oneself-even-unto-consciousness.

The same can be said about freedom. Freedom is a person's ability to determine what affects and surrounds him by changing it or giving it meaning and thereby finally determining his own self. Because I am free, I can react to the illness that attacks me. I can accept it or refuse to be resigned to it. According to the way I react to the situation, I endow my own self with a definite attitude which, in the last analysis, is either love or refusal.

Freedom is a person's power to be a source of changes, of meaning, of his own attitude; hence the power to be also a source for his own self. And here we must say likewise about freedom that it is not merely something a person *has;* for the person *is* freedom. So the being-in-oneself of a person is not only a being-with-himself but it is also a being-"out-of"-himself. The person is not only conscious, but free. Hence to be a person is being-in-oneself in a conscious and free way.

Consciousness and freedom are therefore a flowering of being-in-oneself, of "subsistence," as it is called by the Scholastics. Hence we don't have to make strained efforts to show that there exists a certain form of consciousness and freedom, however feeble it may be, in the lower ranks of visible reality, even in "pre-life." We can content ourselves with stating that they are-in-themselves. True, the lowest forms of beings that are-in-themselves contain something analogous to consciousness and freedom, for these two are not superadditions present in higher beings, but are unfoldings of being-in-itself. However, only the roots of these unfoldings exist at the lower levels; hence we may reserve the terms consciousness and freedom to the level where these reveal themselves in their proper form.

That is why we should like to identify what Teilhard calls the "Within" with being-in-itself. His "Without" would then coincide with what we have just described, viz., dependence on the outside world, being involved in, and at the mercy of the processes that take place in the world, self-estrangement in contrast with being-in-oneself, materiality in contrast with the spirit.

We are justified in saying, without becoming victims of our imagination, that those two aspects can be seen even in the lowest realities of the visible world. Wherever a real unity is present in matter, that one reality is taken up into larger wholes, and consequently is at the same time at the mercy of causes that either build it up or break it down. Yet the reality is also itself and is one. It manages to maintain itself, at least temporarily. Hence it stands "on its own feet," as it were, it is in itself. The crystal, the molecule, the atom, as well as the subatomic particles, are built up and broken down, but they also maintain their own system against attacks from without and tendencies to split up from within. And what we have said about infinitesimal particles, we may repeat about heavenly bodies, about solar systems and galaxies. The two-sidedness of being-dependent on the one hand and being-in-itself on the other, is also proper to the lowest ranks of visible reality, and finds its highest unfolding in man, where we find the two principles of materiality or "prime matter" and spiritual soul.

Lifeless matter and man are respectively the lowest and highest level of the analogy existing in the visible world. Between these two levels are the living beings which provisorily we look upon as likewise constituting one great whole. Hence we disregard here the difference existing between plants and animals precisely because these differences disappear, or rather are not yet manifest, in some unicellular organisms. That is why it is difficult to find terms to express the kinds of activity by which all these living beings manifest their being-in-itself,—namely, terms for the activities that correspond, on their own level, to human consciousness and freedom.

We can speak of the "consciousness" of animals, and even of that of every living being, and contrast with it the *self-*consciousness or "reflection" of man, as is done by Teilhard. In fact, the animal is incapable of reflectively returning upon itself nor can it contemplate its own place in the whole of reality, for this is precisely the capacity that is characteristic of man. To the extent that we can speak of "consciousness" in living beings, it is encompassed by the functions of perception and response. However, we also realize that this process is not a mere chemical reaction to a stimulus. There is a sort of looking things over, a seeing of possibilities, a getting acquainted with circumstances to which the living being attunes itself, in which it will fulfill the pattern of its life, and to which it will respond. This conscious, knowing aspect of the reaction one may call "intelligence," as is done by biologists and animal psychologists, but such an intelligence, of course, is not the same as the "intellect."

Intelligence is present especially in the higher vertebrates. In insects, instinct is the characteristic power. Choice and adaptation are already fixed in instinct, but instinct also differs from a chemical reaction. In both forms, intelligence and instinct, we see a certain activity that distinguishes, compares, and seeks; we observe a non-reflective consciousness. In accord with this is the fact that the activity is not a mere reaction but proceeds from the living being. There is spontaneity which foreshadows human freedom. It expresses itself in a choice within a definite pattern, but there is no true giving of meaning, and still less a formation of an autonomous attitude with respect to reality.

In giving this description, we have kept our attention fixed on higher animals and have not dealt specifically with plants. It was merely our intention to show that being-in-itself grows constantly in perfection as we ascend along the line of the lifeless, the living, and human. In living beings there is a knowingly-being-with-oneself, but they do not yet have a full knowledge of self; they have consciousness but do not attain the self reflectively. They also have an acting-"out-of"-themselves, but they do not yet give to themselves an attitude toward reality as such.

In man being-in-oneself is fully being-with-and-"out-of"-oneself, in self-consciousness and freedom. We see then that there is an ascending analogy in accord with the being-in-oneself which is the active moment of every being. In connection with that, the other aspect—namely that of being-dependent on and at the mercy of the world—is likewise more and more overcome, although it always remains present. Teilhard expressed this in the law that consciousness grows in direct proportion to the increase of complexity. The "Without" is more and more "rolled up" in order that being-in-itself may be more fully lived, and the structure becomes more complex to insure better protection for individual existence.

We believe that in this way we have given a more definite content to the analogy of being, posited by Thomistic metaphysics, with respect to the visible world. That analogy then coincides with the "hyperphysics" of Teilhard de Chardin, at least so long as we abstract from evolution. But, as soon as the analogy of being is confronted with the fact of time, it again leads us to the affirmation of evolution. At the same time, analogy enables us to get a clearer view of evolution. This is the topic to which we must now devote our attention.

EVOLUTION AND MUTATIONS

Analogy means likeness between things but also, inseparable from it and as part of it, difference between them. Hence in the evolutionary ascent there is no mere unfolding of that which remains identical but also, and inseparable from it, a real change, the appearance of a difference, the crossing of a threshold, a "leap." This the first evolutionists, such as Lamarck and Darwin, accepted as a fact, for they spoke of higher species springing from lower species, although they believed that the changes came about gradually. Hugo de Vries, on the contrary, attributed a more explosive character to the changes, in his mutation theory.

Teilhard remarks that the changes appear more abrupt to the modern observer than they really were, because the intermediate forms and the frail beginnings of the new forms have not been preserved. This he calls the law of the "disappearance of pedicels."[21] However, he too repeatedly speaks of "crossing the threshold," when quantitative development issues into something that is qualitatively new.

As everyone admits, true transitions have taken place, although paleontologists mostly postulate a series of small mutations. We may note here that the doctrine of evolution becomes more acceptable to Catholics when the transition from the animal to man is conceived as an essential mutation. They do not have to cling to the second chapter of Genesis in a materially literal sense,[22] but should rather insist on the real distinction between animal and man which is the foundation of man's vocation to a supernatural communion with God.

The question now presents itself whether it still makes sense to speak of evolution, that is, of development *from* the lower, in the case of a mutational leap. We believe that it

---

[21]*The Phenomenon of Man*, pp. 16 f.
[22]Taking everything literally, they would have to say that Adam came forth from clay.

can still be so called, and that the higher, in spite of all its true differences, has its actual origin in the lower. To make this clear, let us recall that the higher, in spite of all the differences and newness that characterize it, nevertheless really belongs to one and the same world: it is precisely *in* that world that it is new and higher.

We are thus brought back to the question of unity and we could repeat here the argument that made us conclude from the existing unity of the visible world to the genetic inter-relation of its parts. But we can also start with the analysis of procreation, of causing something to be. And we could show that in such a process there always appears something that is irreducibly new. Hence we should not *a priori* exclude that the process of causality may lead to something essentially new.[23]

After all, what do we mean when we say that something is caused? A cause is the origin, the source of something, the whole reason of its being, except precisely to the extent that the thing that is caused exists outside its cause and is in-itself. Hence, whatever is caused can be reduced to another as caused by the other, but, it is at the same time new by the fact that it *is*. Thus, whatever comes into being through the influence of a cause contains a duality of the old and the new, of the reducible and the irreducible, of the dependent and the non-dependent or being-in-itself. We see then that the duality of dependence and being-in-itself, proper to being, is found also in "coming-to-be." This is hardly surprising, for coming-to-be is the initial moment of being.

That this is so becomes more evident when we compare the various levels of being existing in the visible world. In the realm of lifeless matter, when we break up a crystal into two pieces, we notice the dependence, for the pieces do not contain more matter than the original crystal. Yet each piece has become an independent system, having its own cohesion and structure. When a molecule is split into two parts, these

---

[23]Cf. Karl Rahner, *Die Hominisation*, pp. 55-84.

parts may be even chemically, i.e., qualitatively, quite different from the original.

We find higher analogates of those divisions in the world of living beings, namely, generation and evolution. It is important to notice the new element that appears in the process of generation, namely, the way the offspring begins its own course of life. This is particularly evident when generation is not a mere division and the offspring thus shows greater individuality.[24] The severed microbe, the new plant, but especially the young of animals show more clearly their new individual character than lifeless beings and, as we have seen, this is due to the fact that their being-in-themselves is conscious and endowed with spontaneity.

Finally, we find the most striking evidence of newness and individual character in the human child, for the child, as a person, is self-conscious and free, he lives and constructs his own being. That is why we are justified in saying that man's spiritual soul, the principle of his self-consciousness and his being-a-free-person, is not the product of generation by the parents. (As we shall explain later, it would be better and more complete to say *"man* as a person, *man* with respect to his spiritual soul is not generated."*) But, just as we find in all living and non-living beings something analogous to the transcendence of the human person and to the spiritual soul that is its principle, so do we find something analogous in them to the fact that the human soul is not born.

Lifeless beings have a principle making them be-in-themselves. As soon as the level of human beings is reached, this principle is called a "soul" or "entelechy." This "soul" may be called the principle of an autonomous way of being in the measure in which there is more individuality. Finally, in man

---

[24]Cf. M. Jeuken, "The Concept 'Individual' in Biology," *Acta Biotheretic*a Vol. X, ½ (1952) pp. 57-86; E. Boné: "Approches biologiques des notions d'individu et de personne," *Nouv. revue théol.* Vol. 81 (1959), pp. 949-966. The well-known cosmological dictum "The parts of a continuum are not beings in act but only in potency" has therefore a more perfect validity as we ascend higher in the line of beings.

the principle is the spiritual soul. In every case, this principle—and the whole being in virtue of the principle—transcends being-caused or being-generated and this uncaused being-in-itself grows in depths and perfection as we ascend on the scale of beings.

The new individual in all such forms of division or generation remains on the same level as its predecessors. In the case of evolution, however, there is, besides individual newness, something that is new qualitatively. Hence evolution shows as it were a twofold leap. If we are open-minded enough to accept the surprising leap found in every coming to-be and in particular in every act of generation, we will not exclude the possibility of an additional leap toward something that is qualitatively new, different from, and higher in nature than its origin.

We constantly witness the marvel of the appearance of new individuals among animals and of new persons among men, who assume control of their own existence and shape it even for all eternity. Hence we should not call it strange, though it is doubly wonderful, when a leap occurs from animal to man, when at one stage of change the young of an animal was actually a man. We leave out of consideration here the question to what extent that higher mode of being manifested itself in this first man.

Evolution, which we are led to accept on the basis of the unity of being that is seen in the temporal succession of lower and higher forms, is not cancelled out by the fact that such leaps are required within the process. A scientist might even add: On the contrary, when we behold the energy that is at work everywhere in the diffusion and variety of the universe and especially in the generation of living beings, we consider it probable that this energy not only produces a development within a particular level but also leaps over the thresholds of such levels.

For the sake of completeness and exactitude, we made a reservation when we spoke about the principle that makes a being be-in-itself. We said it was "non-born." We said that this is true, first of all, of the spiritual soul of man, but that it is true also of the analogates of that soul, namely, the principles of living and lifeless beings. We made that reservation in order to avoid any suggestion that man is composed of two parts brought together, as it were, from two sides. The fact is that from the beginning of his existence man's being is unified, although this unity is bipolar. Of course, we must also maintain the ontological unity of beings lower than man, but there is no difficulty in their regard. On the contrary, we had to prove their two-sidedness rather than their unity.

Because of that unity, found in all the beings of our visible world, man included, we can truthfully say that all of them fully are-in-themselves. This means, with respect to man, that he is personalized even in his body and to that extent "makes himself." This statement applies even to his first coming-to-be, for the personalization which man accomplishes by his deeds is a prolongation and unfolding of a personalization of the body which we can call constitutive. From the very beginning, that is, even in his first coming-to-be, man as a person is not only in himself but he also communicates himself to his body. This is but another way of expressing the scholastic dictum that the spiritual soul, as "form," co-constitutes the body. On the other hand, we must also say that the whole man is born. This we express in ordinary language when we say that the man, and not the body, is the child of his parents. The person is a child and the child is a person. Man is a person on account of his spiritual soul, but the soul informs man's whole bodily being. And man is child and offspring according to the body, and this body is wherever the person is.

This bipolarity may be found analogously in the realms of the living and the lifeless, but it is most important in man. We think that this consideration is helpful in bringing about the reconciliation of materialism and spiritualism desired by Teilhard. We even believe that we thereby overcome in principle the more subtle opposition between evolutionism and existentialism. Both he who wishes to develop himself on the basis of his own freedom and he who wants to emphasize his relationship with the animal can find a meeting ground in that consideration.

However, there may still remain one difficulty in the mind of the reader. Is it really possible for the higher to emerge from the lower? Doesn't such an assertion automatically reduce the higher to the level of the lower? As Teilhard rightly remarks, that difficulty remains only as long as we continue to consider things from the standpoint of the "Without." In the realm of the "Without," we accept the law that there is no gain or loss of mass, and that there is no increase of energy but merely dissipation of energy in the form of heat.

If, on the contrary, we look at the "Within," the aspect of being-in-itself, we witness that the higher, that life, that being-a-person, emerge. That is, we see a growth and increase, or rather an intensification, of being. We must begin by accepting that fact. But this does not mean that the higher has been reduced to the lower or that we should accuse those who accept evolution of making such a reduction by the mere fact that they are evolutionists. As Delfgaauw says rightly:

> We hold that life has indeed developed from the lifeless, and that man has emerged from the living, but in the sense that the higher always springs from the lower. The terms "lower" and "higher" indicate that a new "dimension" is always added to the manifestation of matter: from the lifeless to living matter, from living to conscious matter, from conscious matter to self-conscious or spiritual matter. The paradox here lies in the fact that the higher proceeds indeed from the lower and yet that it cannot be reduced to the lower. Evolution brings forth not apparently new beings but beings that are really new.[25]

---

[25]Delfgaauw, *Het vraagstuk van het materialisme,* Baarn, 1962, p. 10. Cf. Nicolas Corte, *Pierre Teilhard de Chardin, His Life and Work.* New York, 1960, p. 42: Teilhard "was to observe when he mixed in American religious circles that to the Catholics there, evolution was still synonymous with materialistic monism. He was to spend the rest of his life combating that prejudice."

To this someone might object that we have left out of consideration the principal factor, namely, God's creative act. But we should not too readily insert divine action, for in this way we would make God's activity supplementary rather than creative. Let us discuss this matter more fully.

EVOLUTION AND CREATION

There are atheists who look upon evolution as the ultimate explanation of reality. Evolution then takes the place of a divine Creator. We leave aside the question whether Darwin must be included among evolutionists of this type.[26] It is certain that Bergson is not one of them. In his famous work *Creative Evolution,* he nowhere excludes a transcendent Creator from his thinking, although according to him the creative power lies first of all in life, in the "élan vital," and in its highest, i.e., mystical, expression this power resides in the creative love of man.

God's creative activity is explicitly included in P. Chauchard's work that bears the reverse title, *La création évolutive.*[27] It is precisely about this kind of evolutionary creation that we should like to speak here, namely, about God creating an evolving world, about a creation which, taken "terminatively," coincides with evolution—at least if we consider the visible world. But this aim requires that we first discard a too narrow concept of God's creative activity. The idea of creation is strongly colored by the expressions "in the

[26]Charles Darwin was personally inclined toward agnosticism, but he avoided philosophical and theological considerations in his work. At the end of his best known work he speaks of the Creator in a sense which, perhaps dictated by opportunism, is not less true on that account: "There is grandeur in this view of life, with its several powers, having been originally breathed by the Creator into a few forms or into one; and that, whilst this planet has gone cycling on according to the fixed law of gravity, from so simple a beginning endless forms most beautiful and most wonderful have been, and are being evoked." *The Origin of Species by Means of Natural Selection, or the Preservation of Favoured Races in the Struggle for Life,* 6th ed. with additions, and corrections to 1872, London, 1888, p. 429. Cf. P. Overhage, *Das Problem der Hominisation,* p. 202.
[27]Paris, 1957.

beginning" and "out of nothing." We shall therefore try to obtain a more complete grasp of divine creation on the basis of Revelation and reason in order to arrive at the true meaning of those expressions.

Undoubtedly, one of the most powerful expressions of belief in God as Creator is contained in Genesis 1,1—2,4. And yet this first chapter of the Bible is rather a terminus, or at least, one of the crystallizations of the whole belief of Israel in Yahweh, its God. Just as in the New Testament the Apostolic Profession of Faith says first, "I believe in God the Father Almighty" and only after that adds, "Creator of heaven and earth," so was Israel's faith primarily a faith in the God of the Covenant. And it is only within the context of God's historical action as a Covenanter that Israel also recognized His creative activity.[28]

Yahweh is a God who leads his people in history and manifests in it that He also rules over the other peoples and has dominion over nature. When He calls forth men of God in Israel, we see that He also forms them as children in their mother's womb. Especially in Deutero-Isaia, the verb *bara, which* we translate by "to create," indicates first of all the unheard-of fact that God is acting in history by rescuing His people. Only after that does the sacred author show Him at work also by creating "in the beginning."

Similarly God's word is first experienced as operative and beneficient in Israel's history of salvation. And here once more it is only after this that the power of God's word is seen in creation. When God justifies His providence toward Job, he appeals as much to His present work as to what He did "in the beginning." These words of Genesis 1, 1,

[28]We have tried to place the biblical doctrine of creation in that context in our book *Het geloof van ons doopsel,* vol. I, 's Hertogenbosch, 1955. But this doctrine could be developed in greater detail, especially in regard to creation by God's Word. Cf. also, for instance, P. de Haes, *De schepping als, heilsmysterie. Onderzoek der bronnen,* Tielt 1962; G. Lambert, "La création dans la Bible," *Nouvelle Revue théologique,* vol. 75 (1953), pp. 252-281 (summary in *Theology Digest,* vol. 2, (1954) pp. 159-162; Robert W. Gleason, "Creation in the Old Testament," *Thought,* Vol. 37 (1962), pp. 527-542.

therefore, should not be taken in a narrow and exclusive sense. They mean that God's creative activity is the foundation of everything, not that His activity has ceased. Only the Sabbath rest of God at the end of the first account of creation can give that impression. The attempt to base the law of the Sabbath on God's own activity works therefore to the detriment of the view of creation as described in the other books. Hence we are permitted to see a certain rectification in the words Christ spoke after He had cured a man on the Sabbath: "My father works even until now."[29]

Accordingly, God's creative activity, as viewed in the whole of the Bible, is something that is constantly going on. Scripture does not restrict that creative activity and oppose it to the activity by which God sustains, activates and governs the world.

From the standpoint of theological and philosophical reflection we can interpret such a distinction only as expressing two different aspects of God's activity, but we realize that we are not permitted to limit that activity. First of all, there is no reason for such limitation on the basis of God Himself, for He does not pass from one activity to another; in Him there is no succession of separate activities, and all His activity coincides with His being.

Again, when we consider creation in the passive sense, as it affects the creature, we are likewise not permitted to distinguish creation in contrast with other relations, except as expressing a different aspect. For, to be a creature means to be totally dependent on God's transcendental causality.

This dependence means, first of all, to be dependent even in being-in-oneself, which in man means to be a person. For, like any other being in the entire world, we are dependent on God even in that aspect in which, as we have explained, we are independent of the rest of the world. We are also dependent on Him in our continued existence, hence in all activity and passivity, in all causation and coming-to-be, in all we produce and become. God makes

---

[29]John 5, 17.

creatures exist and therefore also makes them remain in existence. He makes them grow, act, cause and be caused.

The relation of creation is, as it were, vertical. It leaves intact all horizontal relations or, more exactly, it precisely brings to reality and permeates these relations. God creates an evolving world, not only at its beginning but also in its full development. God constantly actualizes this world as an evolving world.

We see then that the words "in the beginning" must not be understood in a narrow and exclusive sense. The meaning of God's action at the beginning means rather that He is *before* the world. Better still, since the expression "before the world" puts Him, as it were, in a time before time, it is preferable to say that it puts God above and outside time and the world. That is why the world, in all its duration, in all its unfolding and fullness, has its foundation and source in God's creative act. God creates in the beginning, that is, from His eternity, from Himself, and this relation of God and the world remains always the same.

Creation "out of nothing"[30] can be understood in a similar way. "Before the beginning of the world," using once more this self-contradictory expression, there was nothing; there was nothing from which, by which, or with which God brought the world into existence. The world is totally "out of nothing," that is, it has its complete explanation and origin in God's infinite power and will. God creates it from nothing, with nothing, that is, without pre-existing matter, instrument, or means, purely from himself. Hence "out of nothing" signifies fundamentally God's transcendental causality. It is precisely this causality that is the basis of the whole world with all its relations and events, including the coming-to-be of realities from other realities. From nothing, that is, with complete independence, God creates also the latter realities. *It is from nothing that God makes one thing emerge from the other.* He is the Creator of an evolving world.

---

[30] 2 Mac. 7, 28.

It follows that there is no need to set a limit to God's creative activity in order to make room for evolution. Yet this is sometimes done. It is useful to take note of the ways in which it is done, for it will prevent similar mistakes on our part. There are especially two possibilities. One might, first of all, overrate the "beginning" of the world. We then put everything that is destined to appear later, already at the beginning, so that we can say that it was nevertheless created by God. St. Augustine reasons that way, for, though he says that God created all things "seminally" in the beginning, he also asserts that in their "germs" the various species were already present at that time.[31]

One might also be tempted to say that even Teilhard de Chardin inclines to the same opinion if we take the terms "life" and "consciousness" which he sometimes applies to lifeless things too literally. But, when we look at his vision as a whole, it appears that for Teilhard these terms refer to a pre-phase which is a lower analogate of life and consciousness as we have explained above.

However, the overemphasis on the term "beginning" is not the principal attempt to solve the false problem of evolution versus creation. Generally speaking, it is readily granted that God acts as Creator even after the "beginning." But—and here is the second false solution—a wrong interpretation is often given to that activity, in the sense that God's continual creative activity is broken up into ever new interventions and interferences.

Many philosophers and especially theologians accept such an intervention when an essential change takes place, when there is a real "leap" across a substantial threshold, as in the passage from non-living to living and especially in the emergence of the first men—as also for the origin of every single

---

[31]Cf. especially *de Gen. ad litt.* XVII, 32; ML 34, 406. Cf. E. Portalié, "Augustin (Saint)," *Dict. de Théol. Cath.* I, col. 2349-2355. By the fact that Augustine puts those *distinct* species as present— though it be only in "germ"—at the beginning, we should not call him an evolutionist in the modern sense of the term. Moreover, he also accepts later interventions of God, especially with respect to man.

man.[32] But we believe that it is not necessary to invoke such interventions, provided we conceive God's creative activity with the seriousness it deserves, as we have explained above.

God is always active. It is He precisely who *constantly* actualizes the world in its ever greater unfolding and evolution. This He does at the stage of the greatest "leaps" across frontiers, but His activity is not confined to those stages alone. We are permitted to speak particularly about creation in respect to those critical stages when new forms arise, provided we keep in mind that in so doing we merely emphasize an aspect of God's activity and the creature's dependence which in reality are the same throughout. And the expression creation "out of nothing" also applies to the whole world within which one thing actually proceeds from another.

Those efforts to safeguard God's creative activity are not only useless, but in reality lead to the opposite result. For, if we say that God creates only at the beginning and that His activity is subsequently replaced by other causes, or that His operation intervenes and becomes like a link in the chain of earthly forces, we put Him not above but among earthly causes. He is then active in the world but not in a transcendent way, not as radically above it. Thus, He is no longer God.

To express this in modern theological terms, God as God is always the transcendent and at the same time the universally-immanent cause of the whole world and everything in it. But, as God, He is not a cause in the "categorical" sense, He does not belong to a definite category, He does not effect something alongside other causes that produce something else.

When we say this, we are thinking of God's creative activity and not of His supernatural activity. For, with re-

[32]This is the view of N. Luyten, although he thinks to avoid God's "interference" by attributing to Him a "principal" causality and to the creatures as causes an "instrumental" causality. Cf. his article "Evolutionisme en Wijsbegeerte" *Tijdschrift voor Philosophie* vol. 16 (1954), p. 30. It seems to us that according to that concept the Creator acts at least in a "supplementary" way. See the observation of Karl Rahner regarding the *praemotio physica terminative sumpta* in *Die Hominisation*, p. 68.

spect to the supernatural, God the Son is within our world, but as man; hence this Son (and the Father through Him and the Holy Ghost from Him) also works in a "categorical" manner. God's creative activity, however, is purely transcendental. Hence He does not "supplement" the deficiency of lower causes, but He brings the world to realization in such a way that the higher really emerges *from* the lower.

If God does not create by intervention from outside, the same must be said about the creation of the human soul. We are quite willing to profess the "immediate creation" of the human soul, but we should divest that statement of all dualistic connotations. In our previous remarks, we have tried to eliminate such faulty ideas regarding the existence and the origin of man. The soul is the principle and the "pole" of personal being-in-oneself, and materiality is the principle of being-dependent. No matter how much man is connected with, and dependent on things, he is, as a person, by virtue of his spiritual soul, in-himself, free, and self-realizing. The same must be said about his origin. Now *it is precisely this aspect, as caused by God, that is expressed by saying that the spiritual soul is created.*

The expression "the soul is created by God" means that the soul is the principle in virtue of which man is his coming-to-be is independent of his parents and caused only by God. And again, this holds good not only for man's origin but also for his continued existence.

Hence we should not say that the soul is "infused," if we mean that it is added to an already existing human body. The soul is created "immediately," but in reality all creation is equally immediate, for God is not at work only at the beginning of the world. The relationship of the creature to the Creator encompasses man's entire being. In all non-personal respects, this relationship is accompanied by horizontal relations to, and dependence upon, parents and the surrounding world. However, for man as a person, i.e., according to his soul, this relationship is the only dependence he has in his coming-to-be and his continued existence.

Hence the creation of the human soul is neither more nor less than the beginning of a new person in a whole world, which is constantly created by God as a world in which there is an increase of human persons. And the creation of the souls of the first human beings was the coming-to-be of persons in a world which, under God's creative causality, had reached the apex of its evolution.

We can now complete our answer to the objection that the higher cannot come from the lower. As we have noted, if we look at the being-in-itself of reality, we see the constant appearance of new things, and we see that sometimes the higher springs from the lower. Someone might answer: "Granted—but it is precisely here that God's creative activity plays its role."

As we have said already, such an intervention would reduce God's creative activity to the rank of being a supplementary activity. It should be clear now that there is no need to conceive God's creative activity in that way. We should, on the contrary, exclude that concept because such a supplementary activity, such an intervention and interference, would place God among this world's immanent causes. He would thereby cease to be the transcendent God.

The fact that the higher proceeds from the lower does indeed refer to God, but it does not refer to Him as to a cause which supplies a missing link in the chain of this world's causes. Hence it does not make God's activity an observable phenomenon.

The leap from the lower to the higher, however, points to God's existence and operation just as any other proof for His existence. Any proof for God's existence makes us see a reference to the Infinite. Every finite being, no matter how perfect it may be within its own limits, necessarily contains, we may even say *is,* such a reference to the infinite. This insight can arise from diverse aspects of finite reality. That is why there are several "ways" that lead to the affirmation of God, *among others* the "five ways" of St. Thomas' *Summa Theologica.* One of these ways is based on coming-to-be, and this coming-to-be manifests itself most strikingly in the passing of thresholds spoken of by evolution.

Every newness of a being that exists in itself, outside of its causes, and *a fortiori* the newness of a higher being, shows that this world does not have its ultimate explanation in itself. Coming-to-be looks forward to fullness of being, and the ascent looks forward to the summit on which that fullness is realized. Far from being a difficulty that militates against the existence of God, evolution is a proof for His existence.

In this way evolution leads us to God. At the same time, it also completes our notion of God's creative activity. A static image of the world makes us approach God's creative activity principally from the standpoint of efficient causality and the exemplary causality connected with it. God makes everything as it is; He forms the nature of the things that are and makes them reflect something of His own being; He makes man be an image of Himself, and leaves traces of Himself in the rest of the world.

An evolutionistic image of the world adds something to this picture and makes us see God's final causality within it. God not only makes beings, but He moves them in their ascent. He both propels and attracts them. The ascent toward man is the growth toward God's image. The history of mankind is, at least from God's standpoint, an increasingly clearer and fuller development of that image.

According to the Greeks, "God moves as that which is loved."[33] But the Christian can add: "as He who is loved," for God Himself is the first to love.

Causation in our world—and this applies also to human products and human procreation—is "to put something outside its causes." We have repeatedly noted that what is caused is in-itself with respect to the cause. We can now add that this is the beginning of a being's own development and its growing-apart, of its becoming independent of its causes, as is most strikingly exemplified by birth. The creature, how-

---

[33] Aristotle, *Metaphysica*, 1072, a26.

ever, remains always dependent on God. We are prompted to affirm that dependence, even when we consider merely the static image of creation. But when we consider things dynamically, from the standpoint of the evolution of creation, we must add that creation grows constantly Godwards, though it remains infinitely distant from Him. God's creative activity gives something existence *out* of Himself and *toward* Himself, so that the creature has also an openness for a dialogue with God which totally transcends its own powers.

In the static image of the world, the earth is the garden or dwelling for man, but from the evolutionary standpoint it is his womb and mother. We find the latter image even in ancient mythologies, although the earth is pictured there only as producing vegetation and feeding man. For us the earth with the whole of living nature is the mother's womb which begets us. At the same time, however, the earth remains below us human beings and is therefore more womb than mother. Ancient paganism, on the contrary, put the earth above man and in many agrarian cultures Mother Earth is divinized. The god or gods of heaven have there the father role of fertilization.

Scripture is far removed from such ideas, not only because it has no trace of the sexual debauchery that accompanied the cult of those gods, but especially because it rejects their dualism or polytheism in the representation of the divine. Let us stress the fact that the Bible rejects both those views: the earth or nature is not a mother-goddess and Yahweh is not a father-god; He is not a fecundating god; hence he is not to be represented as a "calf" i.e., as a young bull.

By rejecting these views, the Old Testament did not so much intend to safeguard God's immateriality—it does not hesitate to speak about God's countenance, arm, back, and feet—but rather it wished to express and emphasize His transcendence.

Yahweh is not the father who meets and impregnates Mother Earth, but the Creator who, through His word, gives existence to the earth and even to Heaven. Only when this is clearly established for Israel, can He show Himself in the Old Testament as father by His love. In the New Testament He is fully Father for us, for He sent us His Son, who is with Him in His transcendence and who was with God from the beginning, and He made His Son become man, born of a mother who is God's first handmaid and believer.

CHAPTER TWO

THE ORIGIN OF MAN

Biology describes the individual origin of each man and paleontology tries to trace the origin of mankind. The emergence of human beings especially raises questions regarding the proper meaning of Revelation, but there are similar problems also concerning each man's individual origin. These questions require theological reflection as well as philosophical study. It is principally from the latter two standpoints that we intend to speak in the present essay.

It is evident that philosophical reflection does not give us a graphic account of man's ontogenesis or phylogenesis. The same applies to Revelation. Let us therefore state at once in what way philosophy and theology are nonetheless able to speak about our origin. They can do so by looking at things in retrospect. From the philosophical standpoint we understand ourselves as we now are and we philosophize as mature men. From this we can reason to what our origin must have been, or cannot have been, in order that it could be called the origin of man.

God's Revelation also makes us understand what we are as His children and creatures, and from this also we can try to understand our origin. Let us therefore confine ourselves provisionally to what Revelation and our own philosophical reflection tell us about man purely as man and as creature, in order to draw some conclusions from those considerations.

REVELATION AND THE IMAGE OF MAN

Before beginning our discussion, it is necessary to ask ourselves one question: Does God's Revelation teach us a doctrine concerning man or an image of him? Our first answer can be in the negative. God does not speak *about* man but *to* man. He tells us "I am your salvation." God thereby lets us see what He wishes to be for us and what we are and can be for Him.

Of course, God speaks to men and through men who have themselves particular ideas about man and the world, however un-reflective they may be, and these ideas resound in the human transmission of God's message of salvation. But these ways of looking at things are proper to those men and belong to their own type of culture. These particular views are not the Revelation itself that is offered to us for our belief, but they serve in the transmission of the divine message as a vesture or as a presupposition.

The first chapter of Genesis gives us a well-known example of that fact in the image it presents of the world. The divine message consists in the proclamation that God created the world and especially man. The sequence in which the various creatures appear is a presupposition and a vesture. After all, it differs from the account that is given in the second chapter of Genesis.

What has been said here about the world applies also to man. The whole Bible, as well as Tradition, gives us a message of salvation for man; they do not teach us what man is in himself. Hence we notice that man is spoken of in ancient Israel as a unity and there is not much awareness of the distinction between body and soul. This Semitic concept of man remains the only one that is found in the Bible until the end of the Old Testament. In its last book—namely, Wisdom—and in the books of the New Testament, the Greek concept of man appears alongside the Semitic concept. In later Tradition, it is the Greek idea that is constantly presupposed when man is spoken of. It is characteristic of the Greek concept of man that it makes a distinction between body and soul.

In view of the difference between the message of salvation that is expressed in Revelation and the particular concept of man that is not the matter taught but is merely presupposed, it is evident that the question of the particular image we form of man has no importance for our faith. Whether he is considered simply as one or as composed of body and soul does not enter the message of salvation. Whatever man's make-up may be, God promises him salvation in Christ, and this is the only thing with which Revelation is concerned.

This is a first distinction we must make in order to get a clear-cut view of the problem. However, in regard to man it is necessary to be more specific, for we realize that the question of the idea we have of man is not as indifferent for the understanding and the transmission of God's Revelation as the question of the formation of the earth's crust.

A number of things suggest that Revelation probably says more about man himself than we made it appear so far. There is, first of all, the way we should conceive our final salvation—whether it is a liberation of the soul from the body or the liberation of the whole man in body and soul. There is also the question regarding the way the glorified Christ exists and communicates Himself to us. Finally, there is the question about the way we ought to live as Christians.

As a matter of fact, all this implies that Revelation says more than we have mentioned so far. True, neither Scripture nor the authoritative pronouncements of the Church oblige us to accept a particular philosophical concept regarding man's make-up. They do, however, block any attempt to form an image of man that would misinterpret the salvation God has in store for man as he really is. First of all, since St. Paul, the Church has always opposed the dualistic tendency of the Greek image of man and of the Oriental systems which would prevent us from accepting the resurrection of the whole man, that is also of his body.[1] Those ecclesiastical pronouncements continued into the Middle Ages. We have also the condemnation of the Platonic teaching of Peter Olivi who taught that the rational soul animates the body only indirectly.[2] Hence the soul's relation to the body is not that which Plato described: as a sailor in a boat or as a prisoner in a jail.

---

[1] 1 Cor. 15; Denzinger, nos. 20, 40, 207, 287, 347, 427, 429, 531.
[2] Denzinger no. 481.

On the other hand, we are not permitted to exaggerate man's unity to the extent that the spiritual soul is entirely absorbed in the body both in its origin and its death. That's why the Church teaches that the rational soul is immortal[3] and that it does not come into being directly through generation.[4] Herewith we have mentioned the principal pronouncements of the Church regarding man and indicated the boundaries within which the Christian can philosophize about himself.

It is not necessary to bring forward many proofs to show that a philosophical consideration of man is important also for us Christians. It is important, first and above all, because we are men. Our supernatural privileges do not make us less men. On the contrary, they precisely give us the task of being fully man in the virtue of Christ. That is why we shall also better understand the message of our salvation in the incarnate Word as we grow in the understanding of ourselves as human beings. We shall also find in the philosophy of man a platform on which Revelation and the positive sciences of nature can meet. This is the reason for the philosophical observations we now present.

AN IMAGE OF MAN ACCORDING TO CHRISTIAN PHILOSOPHY

When we spoke of the Greek image of man, we used the terms "soul" and "body." Contemporary authors prefer to speak of "person" and "body" (or rather "corporeity"), and in our opinion there is an advantage in using these expressions. Not because there is no reality corresponding to the concepts of "soul" and "body," but because that *pair* of concepts is apt to suggest incorrectly that there exists an opposition between body and soul.

The body is a concrete reality. So also is the person, for the person is an "I," a "you," or a "he." Both "person" and

---

[3] Denzinger no. 738.
[4] Denzinger, nos. 170, 2327.

"body" designate the concrete reality which is the whole man. Man is a person—this much is clear. But man *is* also body. Of course, it is also correct to say that I *have* a body. In my consciousness and freedom—for example, in the way I accept an illness—I put myself, as it were, face to face with my body. But at the same time it is I myself who am involved: *I* am ill, *I* weigh two-hundred pounds, I wash *myself*. Man *is* also his body, and man, considered also as a person, *has* his body only insofar as he *is* likewise corporeal (hence the modern expression "my corporeity").

In contrast with the body, the soul is not a concrete reality. It is a "principle," a "moment," a "pole"; it is, in scholastic terms, a "being *by means of* which" within the concrete reality or "being *which*" man is. However, it is such a principle within our body itself. The soul is within the body, but not in contradistinction to it. What is distinguished from the soul is not the body, but what we may call the "materiality" of the body, and what the Scholastics call "prime matter."[5] Prime matter is also a pure principle of being and a "pole of being." It is as intangible, invisible and incapable of being imagined as the soul itself, though for opposite reasons. Just as the soul is the principle of being-in-oneself, of the immanence of life, of self-consciousness and freedom, so is materiality or prime matter the principle of extension and divisibility, of being contained and involved, of passivity.

---

[5] The "prime matter" of Aristotle and the Scholastics, particularly of the Thomists, is useful to make us understand the unity of soul and body, provided we conceive it not as a being but as a principle or "pole" found in every material being. Thus understood, the soul and the body are not two substances that are brought together, for the spiritual soul of man—and analogously the "soul" of lower living being and even the "within" of inorganic substances—is not in contradistinction to what we call "body" on all levels of being, but it is in contradistinction only to "prime matter" or materiality. The opposition is therefore one of *two immanent principles within the body*. That is why we shall later describe the transcendence of the spiritual soul not as simply a transcendence with respect to the body but as transcending its materiality. St. Thomas says in that sense that the "human . . . . soul . . . by its power transcends corporeal *matter*" (*Summa theol.* p. I, q. 76, a.l c *in fine*) and that "the rational soul transcends the proportion of corporeal *matter*" (*ibid*, p. I, q. 97, a. 1 c. *in fine*).

Thus, soul and materiality are opposed as two principles within man, but person and body as two ways in which the whole man exists. For, we can say that man is a person insofar as he exists principally on the basis of his soul, and that he is body insofar as he principally exists in his materiality, understood as animated materiality.

A term like "spirit" can designate the human soul as well as the person. The same applies to some extent to the terms "consciousness" and "freedom," as used in modern language. It is hardly necessary to add that the *biblical* terms "spirit" and "flesh" both designate the whole man as respectively saved or enslaved through weakness or sin.

Our principal intention in clarifying these few concepts was to combat the dualistic image of our being-man which finds expression in the distinction between soul and body. This dualistic idea we owe to Plato and even more to Descartes. Aristotle, on the contrary, thought of the soul as an intrinsic principle taken up in the body with prime matter as we have explained. The same applies to the "soul" or life principle of animals and plants.

The Scholastics abandoned the Platonic dualism and conceived the soul as an inner principle of man. The Church likewise rejected a certain type of dualism, as we have already pointed out, namely the kind which admits only a mediate union of soul and body.[6] However, the Scholastics abandoned Platonism only half-heartedly, because they saw no other way to maintain human self-consciousness and freedom, as well as the immortality of the soul[7] and the difference between man and animal. Thus, scholastic teaching, on the one hand, asserts that *one and the same* human soul is immanent in the body, as a principle of being, together with prime matter, but, on the other hand, it affirms that the human soul also transcends the body and exists in itself, is "subsistent," as it is technically called.

---

[6]Denzinger, no. 481.
[7]Denzinger, no. 1783.

Thus far we have avoided the latter proposition in our explanation because it does not seem to have any direct bearing on the question under discussion.[8] We have opposed the human soul solely to the principle of materiality or prime matter and in no way to the body, for we have put the soul in the body. Certainly the human soul transcends something in me, but what it transcends is not my body, for I am my body; but it transcends the materiality of my body. But, one

---

[8]The expression "the spiritual soul transcends *the body*" can be maintained truthfully regarding the body *in its earthly mode of existence,* for in this life the spirit does not yet fully possess the body from within; the body is not yet "eternalized" as an "anthropic" body. Besides, during this earthly life, our spiritual soul likewise has not yet reached its fullness, for it does not yet attain to the full realization of its transcendence of materiality by communicating this transcendence to the body.

Does the unity of body and soul as here described imply their inseparability or can we still look upon death as the "separation of body and soul"? Several answers are possible:

1. The soul and the body are so inseparable that there is no possibility of personal survival after death. This reply is in conflict with God's promises of our eternal fullness. Hence the Church proclaims the fact of personal survival, especially the immortality of the soul, which is individual (Cf. Fifth Lateran Council, Denzinger, no. 738).

2. After the death of the *whole* man, we can expect, because of God's promises, a resurrection which is a re-creation. I cannot see how this reply can be reconciled with the Church's teaching, and how *the same person* who now exists can become a sharer in salvation or perdition if he is first really reduced to nothing.

3. The resurrection is immediately connected with the death of every individual; they are the positive and the negative aspects of one passage to an eternalized mode of existence. This reply is contrary to the *presupposition* underlying the dogmas concerning beatitude, damnation and the purgatorial state. In order not to be contrary to the Church's teaching *itself* about the last ends of man, the reply would have to show how the glorified state of Christ and Our Lady differs from that of the other Blessed in Heaven. One could perhaps say that eternalized corporeity—as indeed the whole man—is not yet completed as long as man*kind* has not reached its fullness.

4. One can continue to adhere to the "separation of soul and body." We can perhaps divest this reply of its dualism by stating that the immortality by which a person transcends the corruption of the body is identical with his (natural) destiny to a supernatural fullness, and that this transcendence is realized in a separation because our earthly mode of existence has come under the dominion of sin and on that account must be abandoned.

may object, can we not say the same thing about the soul of an animal? The reply is affirmative, but in an essentially different way. Every soul, hence every principle of life, in every living being transcends the materiality of that being. And, according to the view of Teilhard de Chardin, which we believe to be correct, the same applies to non-living beings regarding their "Within" in respect to their "Without."

To that extent, then, the human soul has a relationship to materiality which is *like* that of the corresponding principle in lower beings. But there is a *difference* within that likeness, in other words, there is analogy. For the human soul *entirely* transcends materiality. The human soul is the principle of man's personal being-oneself, of self-consciousness and freedom, whereas the soul or the "Within" of lower beings does not raise them to that level. That is why the human soul, together with materiality, constitutes the most individualized and for that reason the most organized of all bodies, the human body, whereas the bodies of lower beings fail to reach that level.

When we observe the corporeal beings of this world, man's supremacy stands out from another standpoint also. Every creature, from atom to man, is dependent upon, and involved in the world in virtue of its materiality. It is constructed as well as broken up by it, for the processes that give rise to one being cause the dissolution of another. But within that stream of change every being maintains itself in virtue of the opposite principle, each one its own way and in varying degrees.

In man, this self-maintenance within the stream of change is characterized by the fact that he has the capacity of remaining "with himself" through self-consciousness, be it only in an implicit fashion, in his dealings with the world. And he can act "out of himself" in freedom within that same stream, be it only to give meaning to the things that befall him.

We could also mention man's immortality, but this point requires a separate treatment. Let it suffice for the present to observe that in my human existence I am myself and exercise this self-possession with self-consciousness and free-dom. But even in this there is an echo of our being-in-the-world, for consciousness is always directed to something that is in the world, it is "intentional"; and freedom always makes decisions regarding something in which we happen to be placed, it is always "situated." Hence the whole man is at the same time a part and a product of a world in virtue of his materiality, and he is also non-caused, free, a person in virtue of his soul. Within the world, then, man, like all creatures, is at the same time dependent and independent, but his independence is the highest.

We say "within the world." But this whole world is God's creation, not merely "in the beginning" if this term is under-stood exclusively in reference to a definite time, but it is always the creation of God. God continually realizes the world and the world is at all times dependent on Him. These relations of dependence or independence of each being with respect to other beings may be represented as horizontal relations, but they are themselves taken up into the vertical relation of all creation to the Creator.

In regard to man, this idea means that he is entirely depend-ent on God, that he is totally creature, not merely that he *was* created at one point of time but that he is *being* created. Man, in virtue of his materiality, i.e., principally because he is body, is also dependent on the world, although those two relations of dependence are not on a par, for God and the world cannot be put side by side. But in virtue of his soul, i.e., as a person, man possesses independence with respect to the world, while remaining dependent on God. Hence from the latter standpoint we can say of man—and even analogously of the beings below him—that he is only "from God."

Later we will speak about the creation of man's soul at the time of his coming-to-be. For the present, we wish to em-phasize the fact that man is continuously *being*-created as person throughout his whole life. Hence man, as a person, in virtue of his soul, is *only* created. As a person, moreover, he can also be conscious of the fact that he is created; he is metaphysically and religiously aware that he is from and by God, this also, of course, within a world. We are thus confronted with a relationship that we shall find once more in the origin of man.

THE ORIGIN OF MAN IN GENERAL

The Church has affirmed the transcendence of the human soul, particularly with respect to our origin and our death. She declares that our soul is created immediately by God and that it survives the disintegration of the body; the soul is not born and it is immortal. The manner in which this teaching of the Church is formulated frequently leads to a dualistic representation of things. The soul is pictured as entering the body at conception, or at the time of "hominization," and it leaves the body at death. This representation can suggest the idea that the soul and the body are only artificially united during our life on earth, a position which the Church rejects. It also seems to imply that the resurrection of the body is merely something given "in the bargain," and this is hardly consonant with Scripture. In short, that representation introduces at the frontiers of our earthly life the dualism which we have tried to discard. That is why it is necessary to examine the Church's doctrine more closely and to change modes of expression which often suggest a dualistic interpretation of the relation of body and soul.

As we said at the beginning, we will start from the consideration of man as we know him to be and then look back to his origin. Provisionally, we describe this origin in a general way, i.e., for individual men and for the first men of our species. In both cases, the Church proclaims the same thing, viz., the creation of the human soul. Let us ask ourselves what this means.

What we said a moment ago about man in his entire existence applies to him, of course, also at the first moment when it is possible to speak of him as a man. Man, in virtue of his soul, as a person, stands in contrast to any influence on the part of the world, including also the generating act of his parents. It is true that every man is the child of his parents, and that means the whole man, not only the body. But this does not exclude, but rather includes, that in his first coming-to-be he stands in contrast to his parents, precisely as a human child, as a person. And so man, the whole man, is at the same time *in*dependent of his parents, because of his soul. And the child does not wait very long before it affirms its own personality with respect to its parents. It makes clear efforts in that direction, even when it is still plainly in need of their help. We find here a sign of the inevitable concurrence of the two relations of being-caused and of being-in-oneself.

This concurrence is even more evident when we reflect upon the coming-to-be itself. Whenever something comes to be, that which comes to be is more than the cause from which it came. The human child, the young of animals, the new plant, the new crystal, the new molecule, are all, each in its own way, a "plus" in contrast with their causes. They are caused, it is true, and have their explanation in their causes, but, on the other hand, they *are* nonetheless, they are outside their causes and independent of them. Hence there arises always something more than what was before. That is why Karl Rahner says that in every coming-to-be there is a *"Selbstüberbietung,"* an "exceeding of self."[9]

This statement is true not only of the coming-to-be that is an arising from something else, but also of the coming-to-be called "growth" with respect to previous stages of development. The child is "more" when compared with his parents, but he also constantly becomes "more" in his growth, especially in the wonderful process of growth in his mother's

---

[9] Paul Overhage and Karl Rahner, *Das Problem der Hominisation. Über den biologischen Ursprung des Menschen,* Freiburg, 1961, pp. 61-84. Cf. P. Schoonenberg, *Het geloof van ons doopsel* Vol. I, 'sHertogenbosch, 1955, p. 163. The twofold moment in the emergence of each man is also discussed by P. Smulders in *Het visioen van Teilhard de Chardin. Poging tot theologische waardering,* Brugge, 1962, pp. 110-119.

womb. We shall say more about this embryonic growth in a moment. Let us now determine how much "more" a child is than his parents.

The child is a new independent being with respect to his parents. He is indeed their offspring, their child, but he is at the same time another human being, a being who has his own being-in-himself. Every new being on a lower level has also its own being-in-itself, whether it is an animal, a plant or an atom. But this being-in-itself is realized in a human child in the highest way: he is a person even from the first moment of his being-man, be it in a dormant though not wholly unconscious state. Precisely as a person and in virtue of his soul, the human child cannot be reduced to his parents. He stands in contrast to them. The same must be affirmed even more strongly about the first men with respect to their animal "parents."

In every coming-to-be of a new man, there is a leap toward a new person. In the origin of the first men the leap was greater because the starting point was on a lower level. This we shall discuss again later. We might wonder at that leap, but there is something to be wondered at in the beginning of any new human life, of any life at all, and even of every new being. As we observe these wonders, we will become more open-minded for the acceptance of the leap from animal to man.

Until now, we have not mentioned God's creative causality. There was no necessity for mentioning it. By this we mean that we don't have to appeal to an "intervention" on the part of God for the creation of the human soul, either at the moment of generation from human parents or at that of "hominization." God does indeed create the soul, or rather, He creates man as person. He creates the whole man and everything else. We can likewise say that God creates the soul "immediately," but He creates everything with equal immediacy. For "to create" refers not only to the first of a series, the subsequent members of which would be reached only mediately, but to the whole series and everything in it.

The procreation by the parents and the origin of the child are likewise subject to the immediate creative causality of God. God constantly creates "out of nothing" a world in which one being springs from another.

In this production of the other, and in its origin and growth, there is always an "exceeding of self," an increase of being, as we have mentioned before. This increase is also from God, and as such *solely* from God. For this reason, we can say by preference that the human soul is created by God. But it should be evident now that this expression does not refer to God's intervention or interference, but is merely a special "aspect" of God's creation of the whole world. We have *no need* to postulate such an intervention, for the Creator does not stand solely at the beginning. He constantly actualizes the whole world with its duration and its growth. Neither are we *able* to accept such an intervention or interference, for to do so is equivalent to an attempt to insert God in the chain of this world's immanent causes, whereas He precisely transcends them.

The creation of the soul of each man is nothing more nor less than the emergence of a new person in this whole world, which is constantly created by Him as a world in which there is an increasing number of persons. The creation of the first man's soul is this coming-to-be of a person in a world which under God's creative causality has reached the summit of its evolution.

THE ORIGIN OF THE INDIVIDUAL MAN

As we said a moment ago, there occurs also an increase of being in the kind of coming-to-be called "growth." This fact is important, if we wish to understand the genesis of the individual man. For, between parents and their offspring, there are intermediary reproductive cells, the female ovum and the male sperm. Before their union, they have a provisional kind of existence of their own independently of the parents' bodies, even before they constitute a new human individual. Nevertheless, they should not be called animal cells, for not only are they the origin of a human being but they also come from human beings. Hence they no longer belong to the animal kingdom in contradistinction to man.

It is commonly said that when the reproductive cells unite the soul is "infused" in them by creation. If such an expression is used, it is important to avoid the idea that a human body exists before a human soul is its intrinsic principle. Moreover, and this is even more important, we must not interpret that creation and infusion of the soul as a divine "intervention." Regarding the reproductive cells prior to their union, we must repeat what we have stressed with respect to the parents, namely, that from them there comes a "plus," a "more," namely, the existence of a new man. Under God's general creative activity, the pre-human reproductive cells become man.

Another question is whether the fecundated ovum constitutes a man from the moment when the sperm and ovum unite. In the Middle Ages, there was an opinion that the human soul appears only at a later stage in the embryonic development. Karl Rahner may be right when he says that today this opinion is gaining ground once more.[10]

One fact especially makes it probable that the fecundated ovum becomes a human being at a later time, namely, the origin of identical twins, triplets, etc. from a single ovum. This fact shows that the fecundated ovum, biologically speaking, is not fully individual, for, though its hereditary characteristics are already determined, it is still possible for the cell to break up and become more than one individual. At least, such a possibility existed in the cases in which the division actually took place.

So long as this possibility remains, the philosophical definition of the individual, "undivided-in-itself," is not yet realized, at least not in the strict sense of individuality as required by the human person. How can we speak of a person, and

---

[10]Paul Overhage and Karl Rahner, *op. cit.*, p. 79.

hence of one who is fully man, if it is still possible for the fecundated ovum to be broken up into two beings which turn out to be two persons? If we adhere to the opinion that the embryo becomes man only at a later stage in its development, on the strength of this and other arguments, we can repeat what we said a moment ago, namely that no soul enters from the outside and that there is no intervention of God.

We may add that this theory of "delayed animation" is not in conflict with any dogma. When Pius IX proclaimed as a dogma that Mary was preserved from original sin from the "first moment of her conception,"[11] everything shows that he meant to speak about the first beginning of her being-human. It was not his intention to determine the biological location of that moment, although the text *presupposes* that such a beginning takes place at the moment of conception.

It is evident from the practice of the Church concerning Baptism that she considers a *born* child as a human being. And the Church also demands that prematurely-born children be baptized.[12] Moreover, she rejects as an excuse for abortion the contention that "animation" comes at a later stage, and especially that "animation" happens only at birth.[13] These practical prescriptions leave open the question of a later "hominization," certainly during the first weeks. Their only purpose is that of choosing the safest course. Moreover, we can also bear in mind that the embryo, even insofar as it is not yet a complete human individual, as well as the reproductive cells, remain human nonetheless since they are, in a certain sense, an extension of the corporeity of the parents.

Whoever speaks of man's origin in his mother's womb refers to both parents. It is perfectly normal and natural for the child of man to have a father and a mother. When we look at it from the standpoint of evolution, however, it fills

---

[11]Denzinger, no. 1641.

[12]Code of Canon Law, Canon 747.

[13]Denzinger, nos. 1184 ff. Concerning the whole question of immediate or mediate animation, see E. C. Messenger, *Theology and Evolution*, London, 1949, pp. 219-332.

us with wonder and raises a problem. The most simple and ancient living beings, so-called "protozoa," unicellular beings, propagate themselves mostly by simple division. Some plants, such as algae and mosses, reproduce themselves by sexless spores. Lower animals, e.g., polyps, can propagate themselves by budding. The higher one ascends in the scale of living beings, the more the mode of bisexual propagation comes to the fore. In plants, there is a distinction of organs, of stamen and pistil with either self-pollination or cross-pollination. In higher animals it is mostly through the mating of totally male and totally female individuals.

However, the relation between non-sexual and sexual ways of propagation is even more complicated than this explanation suggests. Even in unicellular beings, asexual propagation alternates with a kind of contact that can be compared to fecundation. Inversely, there occurs also an asexual propagation by females among higher animals, so-called "parthenogenesis," especially among insects. Katydids propagate themselves parthenogenetically. Among bees, drones have a similar origin. Parthenogenesis is rare among vertebrates. When it does happen, it is almost always artificially produced, that is, by mechanical or chemical stimulation of the ovum.

Is parthenogenesis possible also in man? We cannot wholly exclude it. In 1944, Emmie Marie Jones, a twenty-year-old woman living in Hannover, collapsed in a state of extreme exhaustion as a result of the bombardments. She became pregnant, although she claimed not to have had any relations with men. She gave birth to a daughter, Monica, and her case was scientifically investigated in England in 1955. The daughter was examined—to what extent the examination was thorough and complete, we cannot say—and displayed no evidence of any other hereditary traits than those of her mother. Mother and daughter showed the same hereditary identity as identical twins. However, a transplantation of skin, which is ordinarily successful among identical twins, failed between Monica and her mother. Hence we have here only probability, not certainty.[14]

Let us remark also that, when parthenogenesis occurs in higher animals, as perhaps in the case we have described, the offspring is genetically female. Only some abnormality in the chromosomes, or some hormonal development that affects the chromosomes, can make such an offspring masculine.

We are thus led to ask ourselves: If reproduction can take place in nature in an asexual manner, why do we have sexual modes of procreation? What is the meaning of sexual propagation? Biologists tell us that, when there is bisexual propagation, there is not so much an increase in quantity of offspring as an improvement of its quality. It prevents the harmful effects of inbreeding and, on the other hand, provides innumerable possible combinations of hereditary factors. There arises each time a new variegated individuality, and, in man, it is this rich variegation that lies at the foundation of the variety of personalities.

But there is more than that. In animals, the sexual association continues in a temporary, common care of their offspring. In apes, there is even a sort of choice of a partner, which takes the place of the heat period observed in other animals. Parallel with that, they also exhibit more playful relations with their young. Here we see a foreshadowing of human parenthood, in which the sexual encounter tends to become the embodiment of a personal surrender in love, and in which the long education required for human children has for its foundation not merely the cooperation but the personal community of father and mother.

The Origin of Mankind

When we spoke about the genesis of the individual man, we were tempted to speak about "prehuman beings," designating by that term the reproductive cells before their union

---

[14]Eric Weiser, *Voorplanting van de mens,* adapted and introduced by J. G. H. Holt, Utrecht, 1961, pp. 171-176. For a very critical discussion of the case see W. A. Mijsberg, "Parthenogenese bij de mens?" *Geneeskundige Bladen,* Vol. 48, II (1957), pp. 25-40.

and perhaps also the embryo in the first stages of its development. But, although these "prehuman beings" precede the individuality of the new man, they are within the human species.

Something similar manifests itself with respect to the origin of mankind in general. We have, on one hand, the animals as they are known to us today, namely, the animal kingdom up to and comprising the anthropoid apes, that is, the gorilla, orangutan and chimpanzee. On the other hand, there is man, the *homo sapiens,* who has dominated the earth for some ten thousand years, and who embraces all races that now exist. Between these two, however, other beings have existed which we may now not incorrectly call "prehumans." Simplifying the matter greatly, we can reduce them to three forms: the *Australopithecus,* the fossil remains of which have been found in Transvaal, the *Anthropus*-forms of which the most famous are the *Pithecanthropus erectus* of Java, and the *Sinanthropus pekinensis,* and lastly the *Neanderthal Man.*

These stand "between" the anthropoid ape and homo sapiens according to their type but not necessarily according to their appearance in time. We must note, first of all, that the animal ancestors of mankind are not the so-called anthropoid apes, but both man and anthropoid apes are descended from other and older primates. Again it is not (at least not yet) possible to determine to what extent the so-called intermediary forms follow and descend from each other. Certain discoveries seem to indicate that the homo sapiens was contemporaneous with those anthropus-forms. Nevertheless, it is probable that there were crossbreedings between those forms and, when we put them in the suggested sequence before homo sapiens, we notice a progressive and gradual "hominization" in regard to brain capacity and the shape of the skull, as well as with respect to behavior and the use and fabrication of tools. In one way or another, the ascent from animal to man must have come about in line with those types or forms.

The next question that faces the scientist as he examines those various forms is: Which form still represents the animal and which form represents the first appearance of a human being? The scientists are not sure, but they usually put the frontier betwen the Australopithecus on the one hand, and the anthropus-forms on the other. We are not directly concerned with the correctness of that answer, but rather with the question itself. As Professor Delfgaauw points out, scientists ask this question on the basis of animals and man *as they are known today*. Now those old types and forms do not fall clearly within either the category of animal or that of man. For that reason, following Delfgaauw and others, we have called them intermediary forms.

Therefore, in the first instance, when we start from the phenomena established by science, we witness only a gradual transition from animal to man. Hence the use of the term "prehuman" can be meaningful. But this does not oblige us to give up the question: Is this or that form a man or not? For the same question comes up again in theological and metaphysical speculations regarding the forms which the biologist considers intermediary.

Can we admit that there are degrees in the self-consciousness which affirms one's own being and that of God, and are there gradations in the freedom which determines its attitude toward God? It is certain that there are degrees in their active self-realization, but we cannot conceive that there could be degrees in the self-realization of *being*-a-person. Moreover, it is unthinkable that man, as immortal and as called to supernatural union with God, admits of degrees. Hence man must begin somewhere where he was not before, although it is impossible for us to designate the exact moment with certainty.

On the other hand, it is true that the self-realization of man—even of man as he is defined by metaphysics and theology—can have an endless variety of forms, for man can be everything he makes himself to be. Because we are living in an era of technological revolution and are influenced by existentialist thought, we are getting used to the idea that unimaginable possibilities are open to our being-man in the future. Paleontology invites us to expect unimaginable possibilities likewise with respect to the past of our being-man. Being-human, even in the metaphysical and theological sense, can be "structured" in a way we cannot imagine, but this structure can also be unimaginably low and infantile without ceasing to be human on that account.[15] This makes us realize what problems face us in respect to grace and the sins of the first human beings.

When we spoke of the origin of the individual man, we dealt with human parenthood. When we now consider the genesis of the human species we meet with the lowest grade of parenthood, for the first men had no human but animal "parents." Scripture, however, places before us the story of the sin of our first human parents, and Church authority as well as theology have connected orginal sin with our descendence from them. This brings up the question whether man-

---

[15]Paul Overhage certainly recognizes in the Neanderthal man the same kind of man we are. Regarding his low degree of culture, he says: "This, however, means nothing more than that he had to begin with the most modest endeavors to fulfill the task imposed upon him of conquering the earth and developing a culture, in spite of all the obstacles put in his way by nature. From the beginning he possessed the *full* equipment of spiritual powers and abilities for that colossal task of making world-history, but it was only gradually and on the basis of a long tradition . . . that his ability would manifest itself in ever greater and more refined works of culture *"(Um das Erscheinungsbild der ersten Menschen,* Freiburg, 1959, p. 95, footnote 12). We do not want to assert that these words give us the only possible explanation, but object to Delfgaauw's comment: "This argument comes down to claiming that a child *is* an adult since he is potentially an adult." *(Geschiedenis en vooruitgang, Vol. I, Het ontstaan van de mens,* Baarn, 1961, p. 251). To our thinking, Overhage's idea doesn't mean that, but implies that a child and an adult are both men because the child is potentially an adult. Delfgaauw denies such a being-man which remains identical throughout the course of development: "The human spirit, free self-consciousness, is not a pre-formed capacity which is slowly filled, but the human spirit *is* what it accomplishes" *(loc. cit).* We think it is more exact to say: the human spirit is always a question that looks for an answer and hence is always more than what it finds or executes. Or do those two positions not exclude one another because one is on the ontological level, and the other on the metaphysical plane?

kind as we know it is descended from one human couple, i.e., whether only two human beings had animal parents.

This is a question that comes from theology and which biology does not readily ask itself. A biologist expressed in the following manner the way his science looks at things: "We do not possess . . . a single direct datum enabling us to affirm that mankind certainly arose simultaneously from a number of couples. It is true, however, that science, if left to itself, would probably accept such multiple origin. From what he knows about the origin of most new forms in nature, the scientist is more inclined to accept a 'population' as their starting point. Hence, when the scientist follows his own method and is not influenced by higher motives, he will say that human beings probably evolved by means of 'population' instead of originating from a single pair."[16]

Teilhard de Chardin and others had already spoken in a similar sense. At the same time, however, Teilhard had seen in it an application of the law he had formulated, namely, the impossibility of finding every beginning because of the "disappearance of the pedicels." "That is," he says, "why the problem of monogenism in the strict sense of the word seems to *elude* science as such by its very nature. At those depths of time when hominization took place, the presence and the movements of a unique couple are positively ungraspable at no matter what magnification. Accordingly, one can say that there is *room in this interval* for anything that a transexperimental source of knowledge might demand."[17]

Teilhard wishes to leave the way open for Revelation by mentioning this "trans-experimental source of knowledge." Before we question the latter, however, it is possible for us to point to another similar source, namely, the image of man according to Christian philosophy with which we began this

---

[16]A. Raignier, "De encycliek 'Humani generis' en de evolutieleer," *Streven,* vol. 4, no. 1, 1950-51, p. 274.

[17]P. Teilhard de Chardin, *The Phenomenon of Man,* p. 185, Note 1. Cf. A de Sinéty, Art. "Transformisme," *Dict. Apologét. de la Foi Cathol.,* col. 1948. (This article was written in 1928.)

essay. Is it possible for us to find an answer to the question whether mankind must be traced to one human couple when we look back at the origin of mankind on the basis of the philosophical image we have of man?

Karl Rahner is of the opinion that this is possible and he has given an affirmative answer on the basis of philosophical reasons.[18] Rahner tries to give a philosophical proof for monogenism on the basis of both a "metaphysics of procreation" and God's way of acting. We will begin by briefly discussing the latter point since it will lead us back to the "metaphysics of procreation."

When we described the transcendence of God's activity, we pointed out that we should not think of Him as of one who produced the first men alongside the world's immanent causes, as "creating them in addition." When God produces something in the world, He does it at the same time *from* within the world, by putting into operation the world's immanent causes that are capable of such a production. In other words, He produces men by letting those causes which can procreate do so or rather by making them do it. Does this mean that He can place men in this world only by means of *human* procreation?

At least once, an animal has been able to procreate a man or to cross the threshold that separates man from the animal. Who can say whether or not that kind of causality is unable to operate more than once under God's transcendent causality? We mean, of course, within the frame of favorable circumstances.

God never takes the place of a cause immanent in the world. However, if He again brings a man into existence by hominization instead of procreation, He merely discards one type of causality immanent in the world but not every type

---

[18]See his article "Theologisches zum Monogenismus," in the section "Die Möglichkeiten eines metaphysichen Beweises für den Monogenismus," *Schriften zur Theologie*, Vol. I, Einsiedeln, 2nd ed., 1956, pp. 255-322, especially pp. 311. ff.

within the world, for the hominization of an animal is also such an immanent causation.

Or must we say that God always makes use of the *most* suitable immanent cause? What would force us to believe that? Moreover, is procreation always the most suitable cause? It is true that procreation by a father and a mother has, among other things, the advantage of always permitting a re-grouping of hereditary factors, but does this do away with the fact that a new hominization brings about a much more radical renewal of mankind? Has procreation perhaps a proper and irreplaceable function within the human species so that, when such a species exists, procreation must of necessity be the means for its propagation? We are thus brought back once more to a "metaphysics of procreation."

Every being within this material world is connected with every other being. A book that falls to the ground causes repercussions in the entire cosmos. Everything determines everything in its material structure. Everything cooperates in the construction of what it actually is. Living beings are in no way exempt from that law. They influence and are influenced, even as living beings, for they live in every dimension of their being. They influence and are influenced, moreover, precisely as being this or that kind of being, according to their particular species. This is especially true of the human species. When man is involved in such mutual influences only with the world below him, he cannot truly become himself. He is unable to construct his human person by means of those influences. The fulfillment of the question which man as an embodied person is obtains only in "flesh of his flesh and bone of his bones."

Must we say, then, with Rahner—if we understand him correctly—that the origin of a living being of a particular species, and especially of man, consists precisely in "pro-creation"? It is our opinion that this is so, but only insofar as this being springs from beings of the same species. Or are we perhaps to say: If men already exist, *a human being must of necessity* originate from other men, i.e., by procreation, in order to belong to the same species? But cannot the human species exist also in a "brother" relationship, and not solely in a parent-child relationship? Isn't there also a possibility of being related as men "by way of the primates"?

We are unable to give a definitive answer to all those questions. We believe provisionally that Rahner has given us a description of the ideal origin of every man, rather than of his metaphysically necessary origin. We believe therefore that the question about a monogenetic or polygenetic origin of man remains as obscure for the philosopher as for the paleontologist.

One may ask, isn't it true that Revelation gives an answer to the questions? Doesn't the story of Genesis, Chapters 2 and 3, speak about one couple? The answer is affirmative. However, another question arises here, namely, whether this point belongs to the content itself of Revelation or only to the presuppositions and images of the author. God's Revelation is God's word by which He offers us His salvation. It is not a word in which He gives us knowledge of things that are irrelevant to that salvific message. God explains to us what He is for us and what we are for Him. In this consists the whole content of God's Revelation. It is not His intention to tell us things that we are able to discover by our human powers or to supply knowledge we are unable to obtain by those means.

It is true that Revelation does not refer exclusively to our present *condition,* for it also gives us hopeful perspectives regarding our future and a clarifying insight into our past. However, it does not intend to give us information that does not belong to our personal relationship with God. God does indeed speak to us about our final destiny and our origin. His Revelation is both eschatological and "protological." But eschatology does not supply prognoses about the future, and "protology" does not make up for the gaps in paleontology.

From this viewpoint, the unique couple of Genesis, Chapters 2 and 3, does not belong to the *content* of the biblical message,[19] unless it has a real meaning regarding the sinful state in which we are at the present. Now the doctrine of the Church's teaching authority about original sin thus far has always been expressed in the supposition of a unique couple. Therefore the whole question whether or not Revelation teaches us that we descend from one couple, can be reduced to the question whether this supposition can really be dissociated from the dogma of original sin.

We are unable to answer the latter question. Contemporary theology does not yet attain clarity on this point. Until such clarity is reached, says the encyclical *Humani generis*,[20] it must be presumed that the descent of the existing human race from a unique couple is included in Revelation.

---

[19]For the exegetical viewpoint see Jean de Fraine, *The Bible and the Origin of Man.* New York, 1962.
[20]Denzinger, no. 2327.

CHAPTER THREE

THE HISTORY OF SALVATION

In the preceding essays, we have repeatedly opened the way for a vision that points to Christ. In doing this, we are in line with the ideas of Teilhard de Chardin. He does not look upon evolution as something that came to an end with the appearance of man. Evolution is a process that is going on in mankind, to some extent on the biological plane, but especially in history and the history of salvation.

Biologically speaking, there appear various degrees of development when we compare the anthropus-forms, the Neanderthal man and the homo sapiens of today, although the theory that these *followed* one another and are descended from one another has become very uncertain. Biologically speaking, it is perhaps also possible for man himself to improve the quality of his offspring. But practically no one expects that eventually a superman will arise in the sense of a higher kind of man. Neither does such a superman appear in any way in our Christian perspective, although the question remains whether this perspective excludes the possibility of such a superman.

We must say rather that evolution continues as the fulfillment of man himself, by the fact that he gains an ever-increasing dominion over the earth and attains to an increasingly wider and deeper unity and solidarity with his fellow-men. This means that evolution continues in mankind primarily as history, even on the biological level to the extent that man controls his biological development. Evolution makes progress in a "hominized" way, and this kind of evolution is history.

In fact, thanks to God's gracious salvific will, evolution has even become a history of salvation, and mankind does not attain its final unity and fulfillment except in Christ. This is the vision of Teilhard de Chardin, which he expressed at the end of *The Phenomenon of Man* and developed more theologically in *The Divine Milieu*.[1] We shall now attempt to give a more definite content to that view on the basis of scriptural data.

HISTORY

We believe that we are not doing Teilhard an injustice when we say that his ideas put greater stress on continuity than on discontinuity. This emphasis confers brilliancy and prophetic quality on his vision, but also makes it necessary to fill in and complete the picture. It may be helpful first of all to make a few distinctions. To begin with, there is a difference between evolution and history. In our ordinary way of speaking, "history" means primarily and even exclusively the development that affects men, or groups of men, persons. This is true even when we speak of the history of art, of sport, or of books, for we are then dealing with human products or behavior. We usually do not apply the term "history" to what took place or existed before the appearance of man. And this is even more unusual than the application of the term "evolution" to what is personal. This use of words points to the fact that between evolution and history the same analogy comes into play that obtains between the prehuman and the human, between the natural and the personal. Analogy expresses a certain agreement, and because of that agreement we are permitted to extend the term "evolution" to what is human, as is done, for instance, by Teilhard, and to speak of the history of the prehuman, as is done, e.g., by Delfgaauw.[2]

On the other hand, the analogy expresses a difference precisely in that in which the two agree, and because of this difference we prefer to use those terms in a narrow sense.

---

[1] *The Divine Milieu*, New York, 1960.
[2] Teilhard de Chardin, *The Phenomenon of Man, passim;* B. Delfgaauw, *Geschiedenis en vooruitgang*, Vol. I, *Het onstaan van de mens,* Baarn, 1961, p. 22.

For we have more general terms such as "growth," "genesis," "becoming," "ascent," to express that in which evolution and history agree.

We already notice the difference between evolution and history when we reflect that, in attributing history to the subhuman, we point to "facts" and so presuppose a human consciousness that establishes these facts. The material world has a history only because what happens to it takes place for man.[3] But there is more than that. Only what man brings about with respect to his fellow-men fully belongs to history. For such deeds imply what the word "history" usually suggests: struggle and drama, tragedy and success, responsibility and freedom. Even though this use of the word "history" should reduce its applicability, we wish to point out what is proper to "history" in that narrow sense in contrast to "evolution": *the proper of history is freedom.*[4]

Man makes history by his free decisions, although each individual man has but a small space or opportunity within which he can do so. Every man begins and continues his life within the frame of a definite situation created by the decisions of his ancestors and his contemporaries. That is why it is possible to establish certain laws that operate in human history, at least when we consider it on a large scale, and this is what Teilhard tries to do. We can observe progress in *being-human* within history, although the ascending line —and the same applies to prehuman evolution—is interrupted now and then by retrogressions and there are many developments in dead-end directions.

At the same time, man is free. Therefore, he can fail to appreciate his role in the line of progress and is able to use what his predecessors have developed, to cause his own misfortune and that of others. In fact, the whole of mankind

---

[3] H. Robbers, "Heeft het infrahumane geschiedenis?" *Tijdschr. voor Philosophie,* Vol. 16 (1954), pp. 37-33.

[4] "All those terms, 'becoming,' 'growth,' 'development,' are borrowed from the world of nature. History implies choice, decision; in short, freedom in regard to given situations." A. Dondeyne, *Faith and the World,* Pittsburgh, 1963, p. 160, footnote.

in a certain period can choose such a ruinous course, especially by making a bad choice of powerful leaders. Always, and especially today, mankind faces the choice between further progress and its own—at least partial—destruction. We are certainly growing toward an ever wider freedom of choice, but the question remains whether mankind will make use of that freedom to realize the love and freedom of the children of God. This we must hope for. To hope means to expect something not on the basis of calculation and arrangement, but on that of our trust in a loving person.

Teilhard de Chardin sometimes points to factors in the natural order, namely, the course which evolution seems to follow even in our modern situation, and then again he calls attention to the attraction which God exercises in Christ.[5] The various viewpoints he offers refer to different levels in the one development of mankind. The course of biological evolution continues in human technology and in the direction of greater unity, and this gives us a first foundation for confidence. But it is a shaky foundation, for the course of human evolution is not determined by nature but is a task proposed to the free human being. The law that there is less chance of failure where a large number is involved has only relative value here, for, quite evidently, men are also capable of making an evil choice together and clinging to it in an evil solidarity. On the human level the line of evolution demands a solidarity of love, and the chances for a happy future depend on the opportunity we will allow for love to operate. Hence we must rest our hope more on human persons than on the laws governing evolution and human history.

However, even this human love is not yet the deepest foundation of our hope. The love which every man is called to give to his neighbor is not a purely human love. A first reason is that we do not fully love our fellow creature unless

---

[5] P. Smulders has examined Teilhard's idea critically and developed the same, adding the necessary distinctions, in *Het visioen van Teilhard de Chardin,* Brugge, 1962, pp. 202-232.

we love him in our Creator. The second reason is that *de facto* we are placed in the sphere of God's supernatural salvation, and no love for God or love for man corresponds with our present real order unless it is in harmony with that divine salvific love.

Mankind, and every individual man, must accept or reject the communion which God offers us in Christ, whether he knows that communion explicitly or not. It is only by accepting that kind of salvation that man will be able to produce that love which is necessary to make the world a home for man and mankind a family.

However, the faith that enables us to accept that salvation, and the love by which we live that life, are a gift of God's gratuitous grace. That is why our hope in a beneficent and creative progress of evolution in our history must ultimately rest on the love of man toward man and this love, in turn, must be based on the love with which God in Christ kindles our love and, after a refusal through sin, gives us a chance to restore that love. The ultimate basis of our hope is God's salvific will.

God's Will of Universal Salvation

As we have noted in passing, God's will of salvation extends to all mankind. "God our Savior . . . wishes all men to be saved," says St. Paul.[6] Since he says this is an exhortation "that supplications, prayers, intercessions and thanksgiving be made for all men,"[7] it is possible to interpret the words "all men" in a global sense without precisely referring to every individual. Moreover, to the words "be saved" the Apostle adds "and to come to the knowledge of the truth," and it is evident that he looks on these two as one, i.e., men are saved by coming to the knowledge of the truth, hence by the preaching and the acceptance of faith which introduce them into the Church.

---

[6] 1 Tim. 2, 4.
[7] 1 Tim. 2, 1.

Nevertheless, we are permitted to understand the words "all men to be saved" in a broader sense, as referring to every man, no matter where he is, even if he is outside the Church and has not come in contact with any preaching of God's message. This we are permitted to do, because God's universal will of salvation is evident from the whole of Scripture. We say this not so much on the basis of individual texts, but rather in the sense that God's universal will of salvation is manifest in the scriptural image of God and Christ. Hence the reason for speaking of a universal salvific will of God in respect to the text we have quoted rests principally on the words that follow that quotation; namely: "For there is one God, and one Mediator between God and men, himself man, Christ Jesus, who gave himself a ransom for all, bearing witness in his own time."[8]

This testimony begins to unfold in the Old Testament.[9] True, in the Old Testament, God's activity and salvation are rather exclusively addressed to the small people of Israel. There are scarcely any texts, and certainly no clear words, expressing that God *at the same time* reveals Himself to "the nations" for their salvation. But God's salvific activity is universal in the history before Israel, from Adam to Melchisedech,[10] and particularly after that in the Messianic future.[11]

When late Judaism carried the divine message beyond its borders, it aimed at admitting the pagans as God-fearing men and as proselytes into its own fold. In the book of Jona we read that the Ninivites were converted at the word of a prophet of Israel. It is certainly not clear from the Old Testament that there are also possibilities of salvation for those to

---

[8]1 Tim. 2, 5 ff.

[9]For a greater development of this point on the basis of Scripture and Tradition, cf. P. Schoonenberg, *Het geloof van ons doopsel,* Vol. 3, 's Hertogenbosch, 1958, pp. 195-203. Bibliography on page 195. We refer especially to the stimulating works of Jean Daniélou (though they are sometimes excessively stimulating in the translation of some passages of Scripture). *Le mystère du salut des nations,* Paris, 1946; *Le mystère de l' Avent,* Paris, 1948; *Holy Pagans in the Old Testament,* Baltimore, 1957.

[10]Gen. 2-14.

[11]Cf. especially Is. 19, 22-25.

whom the preaching of the message has not come. The same must be said, at least with respect to the principal point, about the books of the New Testament.

Here we find the fulfillment of the universality fore-shadowed in the Old Testament. The wall of separation that existed between Israel and the nations is removed.[12] In its stead, there now appears, in respect to salvation, the clear-cut separation between believers and unbelievers.[13] Faith is linked with preaching,[14] with baptism,[15] and therefore with the Church. Hence also in the new Testament God's work of salvation is not known outside the confines of the Church and beyond the range of the preaching of the Word. Not quite, however, for St. Paul speaks a few times about the pagans in a way that makes their situation somewhat similar to that of the Christians.[16] These few texts, however, are not per-fectly clear.

Hence, under the new as well as the old Dispensation, the principal foundation for our belief in God's universal salvific will rests on God the Father Himself and His incarnate Son. God's universal will of salvation was made visible in Christ, for He is the only Mediator between God and men,[17] the gift of God's love to the world and therefore the Savior of the world,[18] the One for whom and in whom all things were created, in whom all things hold together and through whom all things should be reconciled to Himself.[19] This image of Christ is perhaps the main driving force behind the theological development of that point.

St. Paul started his speech in the Areopagus by saying that the pagans unknowingly worship the same God as the Christians. In the second century, the martyr Justin, one of the apologetical writers, extends this idea to the *Logos*. In his

---

[12]Eph. 2, 14.
[13]Mark, 16, 16; John 3, 18.
[14]Rom. 19, 14.
[15]Mark 16, 16; Eph. 4, 5.
[16]Acts 17, 23-30; Rom. 2, 13-16.
[17]1 Tim. 2, 5.
[18]John 3, 16; 4, 42.
[19]Col. 1, 16 ff.

two Apologies he argues that the Greek thinkers, such as Socrates, were led by the *Logos* just like the prophets of Israel, and were to that extent already Christians. However, it is not at all clear whether he means by "Logos" the divine Person of the Word or human reason. Or, to express it in our own terms, it is not clear that he refers to a supernatural, (pre)Christian participation in salvation or merely to a mirroring of God in our natural, human insights. It is probable that Justin did not put the question in that particular way, but the problem came to the fore in the Church's encounter with Pelagianism. According to Pelagius, what man has as his own by nature is identical with what Christ brings in the form of grace and salvation, for He merely gives us His example to facilitate what we can achieve by our own efforts.

In opposition to that doctrine, St. Augustine, and after him the Councils of Carthage and Orange, clearly assert that salvation and the entire road to it is a supernatural gift of redemption. Because of the emphasis that was thus put on the gratuitous and redeeming character of God's gift of salvation, the view of its universality which began to come to light in the apologetical writers was once more obscured. Augustine does indeed know a "Church from the time of Abel," but it is a Church of those who are saved from among the *massa damnata* on which grace had been wasted since Adam's Fall.

However, what Augustine had thus narrowed down was gradually opened up again by tradition. The Church of Gaul soon rejected the idea that God destines some to salvation and others to damnation.[20] Later on, the possibility of Christ's grace being operative outside the visible frontiers of the Church was held open against the teachings of Jansenism.[21] The Church's teaching authority has been content with rejecting the denial or the limitation of God's universal will of salvation. It is within this frame that theology endeavors to voice what the believing heart is prompted more and more to profess, namely, that God wants all men to be

---

[20]Denzinger, nos. 200, 318, 322.
[21]Denzinger, no. 1295.

saved, even those who have not yet learned anything about the message of Christ.

The development of this view in biblical and postbiblical tradition rests ultimately on a contact with God, with His love and fidelity, His mercy and salvation, with His Christ. Men first conceived God's love as an election and only later as characterized by universality. This way is very natural to man. The more profound and total our love, the more restricted the number of persons on whom that love can be bestowed. This is the very foundation of monogamous marriage. Thus, when we think of a gratuitous community of love, we are prompted spontaneously to conceive that love as exclusive, even if it concerns God's love. But this restriction precisely does *not* apply to God's relations with His creatures.[22] Although His love for men is gratuitous and His choice and election are free, it has no exclusiveness but extends to all.

Israel and the Church have had to learn the universality of this love through contact with God. However, contact with men who live beyond the horizon of the people of God also has contributed to it. To the extent that we realize that those men are fellow creatures of the same God, we are increasingly ready to acknowledge His love for them. That is why we observe the beginning of a universal expectation of salvation in the Old Testament at the time of the Babylonian Captivity. And God's will of universal salvation becomes self-evident for our time in the New Testament, now that we know that we are part of a human community whose home is the earth and whose life has covered half a million years. Moreover, we appreciate more and more the irreplaceable value of every human person and realize at the same time how greatly the person is threatened by the forces we ourselves have created. We are democrats and don't want any privileged class even in relation to God and certainly not for eternity.

---

[22]We may perhaps say that love has that one-to-one character even in the interpersonal love within the Divine Being. If so, it is found between the Father and the Son, and the Holy Ghost is their love-in-person, their we-in-person.

All that we have said until now strengthens our belief that God earnestly and really desires the salvation of all men and of every individual. But we must also look critically at our democratic way of thinking when it concerns our relations to God.

First of all, our relation to God is not one of justice. And because God's salvific will is universal, it does not thereby cease to be personal and gratuitous. If we wish to have an understanding based on faith of our relation to God, we must rely not so much on our democratic ideal as on the fact that lies at its foundation, namely, the irreplaceable and equal value of every human person. This personalism will seek to find expression within a particular society in a system that gives every man the same opportunities and the same rights.

But such a system can operate only if we suppose that those persons we call equal are at the same stage of historical development. That is why we do not attribute the same political rights to children as to adults, to men who live in the stone age as to those who can maintain themselves in a world-encompassing culture. All persons of the human community are truly equal in all times and places, but their being-a-person is realized differently according to times and places. There is no contradiction between personal equality on the one hand and inequality in regard to place and time, for it is precisely proper to our human person that it develops itself in history. It belongs to our nature to be a person who realizes himself in history.

This idea is fully evident in the fulfillment of God's universal salvific will. God offers his salvation to every man, but to each in his historical situation. The receiving-of-grace-in-Christ, just as being-man, is realized in diverse ways according to time and place. Hence, the possibility of a historical ascent is not excluded but rather included, and within that ascent we shall observe the characteristic tension and interplay between the groups that are advanced and those that are retarded.

70

It is not by taking a snapshot of some democratic state but by looking at mankind as a whole that we shall discover the working of God's universal salvific will. We shall see it at work in a universal history of salvation, which contains unimaginable possibilities both in regard to the past and the future.

This idea brings us back once more to the history of salvation, which we shall now try to trace in broad lines. First, however let us draw attention to one point. We saw a moment ago that God's work of salvation, as recorded in Sacred Scripture, almost always restricts God's salvific work to the area in which that salvation is preached. This is a restriction, but it contains also a positive element. Faith is necessary for salvation, specifically faith in a message: "He who comes to God must believe that God exists and is a rewarder to those who seek him."[23] "But how are they to believe him whom they have not heard? And how are they to hear, if no one preaches? . . . Faith then depends on hearing and hearing on the word of Christ."[24]

The connection between those two seems therefore to be the reason why Scripture never, or scarcely ever, considers salvation outside the reach of preaching. This connection is also true and valid for us, since we are not dealing here with a law which God can arbitrarily make or abolish but with a necessity flowing from man's nature.

One of the reasons why the Sacred writers of the Bible do not easily discern God's will of salvation for all men may lie in the fact that they view man as a unit rather than as composed of body and soul. Theologians at a later time thought of salvation as offered to man's soul; hence they could abstract from the way man bodily encounters salvation in his world. Hebrew writers were unacquainted with this sort of abstraction. It is only during the past few decades that theologians have begun to show interest in this encounter and to find its description in the science of comparative religion. This has

---

[23]Hebr. 11, 6.
[24]Rom. 10, 14, 17.

71

made them realize that non-Christian religions might perhaps contain a message of salvation which men can accept with faith.

Accordingly, if we consider it necessary to go beyond and, as it were, break through the restrictive way Scripture presents things, it is precisely at this point that it must be done, namely, in the sense that God's salvific dispensation extends beyond the preaching *emanating from Israel or from the Church*. However, this dispensation does not extend beyond the preaching or proclamation of the divine message in any of the forms this preaching may take. We shall find this preaching most explicitly in the religious traditions and rites of men. That is why the general history of salvation which we shall now try to sketch is also a history of religions from the time that man began to express his relation to God by means of religious signs.

GENERAL HISTORY OF SALVATION

The history of salvation unfolds within the general history of mankind, but it is not the mere result of the human forces that are at work in this history. The history of salvation is immanent in human history but also transcends it, it is *supernatural*. For, over and above man's free activity, there is also the special activity of God Himself and in particular the fact that God gives ever new opportunities to man's free initiatives. Prehuman evolution and human history are totally under the influence of God's creative causality, although He does not intervene and work alongside the world's immanent causes.

In His supernatural communication God does not act as a cause; He gives Himself personally—ultimately, through the incarnation of His only-begotten and eternal Son. That is why this salvific activity has its privileged points of contact which to a certain extent are independent of man's level of perfection: the Christ comes from Israel and the Church comes from Christ. That activity is displayed in ever new initiatives, even when the preceding situation is not a preparation for it; God exalts the lowly, and His strength first reveals itself fully in our weakness.[25] God's activity operates even when there is an obstacle in the way; He forgives sinners: "You also at one time did not believe God, but now have obtained mercy by reason of their unbelief, so they too have not now believed by reason of the mercy shown you, that they too may obtain mercy. For God has shut up all in unbelief, that he may have mercy upon all."[26] The best evidence for these ways of God's activity is the fact that God gives life through the death which was caused by sin: Christ "is foreordained Son of God by an act of power through His resurrection from the dead."[27]

Taking as our starting point this view of faith concerning the history of salvation, we can try to discover this history throughout human history. For this purpose, we shall now divide human history with respect to salvation and distinguish roughly four phases.

First Phase. First in the order of time is the phase in which we know by faith that a history of salvation is at work though we do not perceive any signs of it. Revelation, beginning with Chapters Two and Three of Genesis, does not give us any information that has been transmitted from the first years of mankind. We have no record, no "reporter's coverage" from that time, as Karl Rahner[28] expresses it. What Revelation does is to make us look back to the beginning with a belief in God as bringing salvation to all. That is why for the time being we content ourselves with affirming that God gave grace to man from his very

---

[25]Luke 1, 52; 2 Cor. 12, 9.

[26]Rom. 11, 30-32.

[27]Rom. 1, 3.

[28]Karl Rahner, "Die Hominisation als theologische Frage," in Paul Overhage and Karl Rahner: *Das Problem der Hominisation. Über den biologischen Ursprung des Menschen,* Freiburg, 1961, pp. 32-42. Rahner develops the same theory more fully in relation to eschatology in "Theologische Principien der Hermeneutik eschatologischer Aussagen," *Schriften zur Theologie* Vol. IV, Einsiedeln, 1960, pp. 401-428.

beginning and that there was included in it in some shape or form a human reply, a Yes or No. We shall return to this point in a moment, though only to state more explicitly that we are not able to say more about the first and longest period of human history. Let us now proceed and take a bird's eye view of the next periods of the general history of salvation.

Second Phase. It is customary to divide mankind's prehistory according to the principal materials used in the production of tools—stone, bronze and iron. For our study it is more important to find out what man did with those tools and how he fashioned his existence through his labor. We thus reach a turning point in human history, which roughly coincides with the beginning of the Neolithic period and which can best be compared to the impact of the technological revolution on our present time.

We are referring here to the transition from a life dependent on the gathering of wild fruits and hunting to a culture that domesticated animals and cultivated the land. It is only then that man began to subjugate the earth and give a new shape to his life as a farmer. He settled in permanent dwellings, villages and towns, he began to divide labor, and laid the foundation for culture, organization, classes and government.

It is principally in such agricultural civilizations that the history of salvation began to express itself in signs. The specialization of human activity also brought with it a form of worship as a proclamation and celebration of God's action toward man and the expression of man's answer. There was a development of holy seasons in the year, of feasts, sacrifices, consecrations and prayers. There were temples and priests, a sacred tradition and sacred writings.

Those signs of primitive humanity, as well as those of present-day non-Christian religions, are not wholly beyond interpretation by us, who have been given the grace of Christ. We interpret them to the extent that those foreign cultures are accessible to us and to the extent that man's relation to the God of his salvation can become clear to others and to himself.

In this sense we see that in those cultures God does "not leave Himself without testimony"[29] and that man seeks and finds his salvation in Him. But we see just as clearly man's tendency to usury his being "like unto God,"[30] he tries to control the divine by his own power and embody it in human ways of life.

On the plane of the history of salvation everything remains the same in these agricultural civilizations, except one point: the dialogue with God now takes on a certain form within earthly activities, namely, that of worship, in the widest sense of the term, of religion as a form of life that manifestly develops alongside the service of man's proper existence. The whole of human life is renewed by this new factor, as appears clearly from the great role played by religion in the life of the men of ancient cultures. Everything bears the mark of man's relation to God, although this very relationship is provisionally an inextricable mixture of his acceptance and refusal of God's offer of salvation.

Third Phase. God, however, personally brings clarity in this confusion, in the little nation of Israel. Up to now we have seen the history of salvation mainly as implied in human history. Its presence remained indiscernible as long as the human person himself did not give voice to the deepest roots of his being, but became distinguishable as soon as man began to express his innermost being.

In Israel, however, we witness directly the salutary initiative of God Himself. He makes Himself clearly known as the only, the true, the personal God, and He brings about the miracle of a monotheistic belief that persists and triumphs in that small people in spite of the pressure of the higher cultures that surround it.

Israel's religiousness is that of a pastoral people and it assumes the forms of an agricultural civilization, but those

---

[29] Acts 14, 16.
[30] Gen. 3, 5.

75

forms undergo a purification and transformation under the influence of Israel's faith in the living God. In the Old Testament, everything is the same as in the Semitic religions, save monotheism, and this makes everything different and new. Faith and confidence based on God's historical deeds, awareness of sin, salvation and judgment, sobriety in worship, and an increasing predominance of the service of the word over that of sacrifice are some of the characteristics of Old Testament religion.

We may limit ourselves here to this summary, characterizing everything in the above-mentioned words: God brings clarity.

Fourth Phase. After the clarification granted to Israel, the history of salvation finally brings us the fullness in Christ. Only now does God utter His eternal Word to us by the fact that the Word becomes flesh. And with it He gives everything: His Spirit, adoption as His children, redemption, and eternal life. In line with what we have said about the relation between the Old Testament and Semitic religiousness, we can now state the following: The religion of the New Testament is the same as that of the Old, save for the presence of God's Incarnate Son, and this makes everything different and new.

This presence ushers in the greatest transition in the religious history of mankind, and this transition is permanent, for it is definitive. God's Revelation is thereby closed or rather completed, since the Father has given everything and, above all, has given Himself completely in Christ. That is why we now live in "the fullness of the times" and in "the last days" though these "days" may last centuries or millennia. All this doesn't mean that history, and especially the history of salvation, has ended. It does mean, however, that that history has as its one and only content the breakthrough of the fullness that Christ has brought and the actualization of this newness in the whole world and in our whole human existence.

Therefore, what follows this history can be nothing else than the absolute fulfillment in which that fullness will be revealed without the darkness of faith and struggle with sin. This *terminus of the history of salvation and of all history, the "Point Omega," is "God all in all" for all eternity.* At this point again everything is the same but, at the same time, because it is openly revealed and fulfilled, all things are new.[31]

There is, then, a history of salvation that goes on indiscernibly, a history of salvation that manifests itself in human religiousness, next a history of salvation in which God brings clarification, a history of salvation when God grants fullness, and finally a fulfillment in eternal clarity. In other words, there are, in succession, anonymous religiousness, paganism, Israel, Christianity, and the final fulfillment. These are the stages in the history of salvation that unfold on the divine and human plane and are immanent in human history, which is itself a completion of prehuman evolution.

When speaking about evolution, we showed the analogy existing between the successive phases of development and the accompanying necessity of leaps over thresholds. We likewise observe an evident analogy between the above-mentioned phases of the history of salvation. For we always find once more in every stage all that we see in the one that goes before, but as made new by an added difference. That is why there are, here also, leaps over thresholds, and on the plane of the history of *salvation* these leaps are seen to surpass those that occur in biological mutations. We saw that the ascent in evolutionary development was achieved under the one transcendent causality of God as Creator. But in the history of salvation we witness ever new initiatives of God's self-communication, we behold an actual advent of God, a coming of Christ.

This advent is most evident in the incarnation of the Son of God, who "came down from heaven" as we say in the Creed. His Second Coming can rightly be called the

------

[31]Cf. Apoc. 21, 5.

manifestation of the presence He has had in us since the Incarnation. However, precisely this manifestation which puts an end to all coming-to-be and struggle, which removes every veil, is the greatest leap ever in evolution or history, precisely because evolution and history, even the history of salvation, come thereby to an end in their eternal fulfillment.

One may notice that the various historical phases we have contrasted and delimited are not distinguished from one another on the same basis. The second phase is distinguished from the first on the level of cultural history, but the others are divided on the plane of the history of salvation. On the level of the history of salvation, the stage of anonymity and that of manifest religiousness merge, which is why Scripture lumps those two together in the series of accounts given in the first half of the Book of Genesis (Chapters 1-11). Conversely, from the standpoint of cultural history, there is no difference between the agricultural types of civilization and Israel, except in respect to what is due to God's initiative of salvific activity.

So the distinctions we have made were based first on human development, and after that on God's self-communication. At first the human and natural served as a principle of division, but later it was the supernatural.

We readily admit that our division is susceptible to improvement. We have, however, some reasons for defending it. A single basis can be kept throughout when a division concerns a reality that remains univocal. When, however, the various parts of a reality are analogously related to one another, and certainly when we are dealing with a growing reality that unfolds in an ascending scale by analogous steps, the principle of division should likewise have only an analogous unity.

With respect to the totality of the visible world, the relations between non-living and living beings on the one hand, and those between living beings and man on the other, are once more mutually analogous. Hence they are both identical and different: the leap toward man brings with it more novelty than that from non-living to living. Looking at the history of salvation, we see clearly a similar analogous ascent in it. This ascent is accomplished by transitions exercising an ever more profound influence on human life, yet there remains also a sameness between the successive phases.

This analogy is already noticeable when we compare the call of Abraham or the Sinaitic Covenant to the Incarnation of the Son of God. Hence it is not to be considered strange if we place before the call of Abraham a change on the plane of cultural history, that is, in the realm of the human and natural. Moreover, the transition from the first to the second phase in our division contains something that is truly important for what follows, because it foreshadows man's relation to God, spoken of by the Old and New Testaments. It is true that this transition is accomplished within the human and natural sphere, but this, like everything that is human, is integrated in our supernatural relation to the God of our salvation. Man in fact, precisely because of God's universal salvific will, is never exclusively natural in relation to God, but he is in everything either positively or negatively directed toward God in a supernatural fashion.

That is why the new cultural situation of the Neolithic Age has a supernatural significance: it opens up the possibility of living in a new and explicit fashion according to man's supernatural relation to God or of rejecting it. Conversely, every supernatural factor is also natural and human. New possibilities were introduced in our human existence by the election of Israel and the coming of Christ. We are therefore permitted to say that the history of salvation has advanced through transition whose supernatural character increasingly manifested itself in the human element.

Let us now add a few words to bring out more fully the particular characteristics of those various phases. This we shall do from the theological standpoint and principally on the basis of Scripture. The Old Testament cast a glance backwards at the first period of the general history of salvation, but also looked beyond its own frontiers at the contemporaneous development of religions in the peoples belonging to the agricultural type of civilization. This Scriptural view we shall try to develop with the help of some anthropological data, but especially by broadening it and making it more positive on the basis of the more profound contact with the God of our salvation given us in the New Testament.

THE ANONYMOUS BEGINNING

The transition from animal to man, when seen through the eyes of the biologists, apparently came about in a gradual way. Between the animal ancestors which modern man, the homo sapiens, has in common with the anthropoid apes, there are clearly three transitional forms: the Australopithecus, the Anthropus-types and the Neanderthal. This does not mean that they and the homo sapiens have evolved chronologically in that sequence and still less that they are directly descended from one another. It is true, nevertheless, that those three intermediary forms represent a transition from the animal level to modern man, when they are considered from the typological standpoint, in regard to body structure and the use of tools. When we study them from the biological viewpoint and from a corresponding phenomenological standpoint, we may say that those transitional types are neither animal nor man, i.e., they are neither animal nor man as we know them today. From that standpoint, therefore, they are truly intermediary types.

We cannot stop here when we view the matter from a metaphysical or theological standpoint. For theology, man is endowed with immortality and has a vocation to eternal happiness. We cannot conceive how these can be more or less present. That is why the theological question comes up, namely, which one of those types marks the true beginning of man. This is an important subject in our present study, for that beginning coincides with the beginning of the history of salvation and it is *possible* that a more definite determination of that beginning might reveal a little more about the concrete beginning of the history of salvation.

However, the question we have just formulated can be answered only by guesses. The rare fossil remains of bodies and the few discovered artifacts give no foundation for a certain conclusion. It is possible that the Neanderthal man and even the Sinanthropus Pekinensis were already men in the metaphysical and theological sense of the word. In that case, we must say that their religious life was inconceivably primitive. Even if only the homo sapiens is a man in that sense, we do not know much more about the beginning of the history of salvation. True, the ascent of the homo sapiens was accompanied by signs of true culture, but we don't know what his condition was before he began to oust the other groups.[32]

---

[32]Rudolf Fattinger, in his book, *War der Adam des Paradieses der Urmensch? Lösungsversuch der paläontologisch, biblisch chronologischen Schwierigkeiten,* Linz, 1961, defends the view that the general history of salvation begins only after a real development which mankind had to attain in order to be able to make an ethico-religious choice. This theory fully deserves a closer theological examination.

It is a pity, however, that Fattinger seeks to prove his thesis by divorcing the historicity of Genesis, Chapters 1-11, from the literary genre of those chapters, the genre of etiology, that is, of a backward glance at the origin of existing reality. Fattinger points out that those chapters are imbedded in a world of agriculture and cattle-raising, which cannot be that of the very first men, but belongs, at the earliest, to the Mesolithic Age (page 10).

He is right in this. But from that etiological character we are not permitted to conclude that the accounts of Genesis also contain exact historical pictures, even though their content constitutes a history of salvation. In other words, the background of those accounts show us that the writers and their sources belonged to a civilization of cattle-raising and agriculture, but it does not mean that the personages that figure in those stories belonged to that type of culture.

Similarly the ages of the patriarchs are borrowed from ancient sources and on that account they too belong to a style of expression and not to what Genesis intends to affirm.

It follows that it is not true that "The Bible must be considered right when it records a few thousands of years" (p. 6).

One may ask also whether the accounts of Genesis are coherent among themselves in regard to their cultural background. Did the history of the culture which Fattinger finds in Genesis, Chapters 1-11, actually take place within the relatively short period of the biblical chronology?

That's why we believe that there is no need for this sort of concordism. The theory that the history of the salvation and condemnation of mankind begins only in the Mesolithic Age is neither proved nor disproved by the chronology of the Bible. This question should be judged by examining whether the complete sources of Revelation oblige us to hold that original sin was already strictly universal from the beginning of mankind.

For it seems possible that the homo sapiens was already contemporaneous with the Sinanthropus.

Hence in any hypothesis, we can only say that the religious beginning of mankind was inconceivably primitive. We use the term "inconceivably" on purpose. It is likewise not possible for us to draw conclusions from the study of children with regard to the time when mankind was in its childhood, for the child of today is in every respect situated in a culture which has been built up during half a million years. The essence of man contains historical possibilities which are inconceivable for us at present. This is true not only with respect to the future in proportion to its distance from our present, but applies also in the same sense to the past.

But, one may ask, doesn't Revelation tell us more about the existence of the first men? Don't chapters Two and Three of Genesis give us a description of their concrete relation with God? To both questions we must reply in the negative. God's Revelation is God's word by which He offers us His salvation. It is not a word in which He gives us knowledge of things that are irrelevant to that salvific message.

Hence the writer of Chapters Two and Three of Genesis gives us nothing more than these important facts: God offered man His supernatural salvation in the first phase of his beginning, and from that very beginning there was both sin and grace in the world. The writer clothed this retrospective view in forms and images that were familiar to Israel's concept of God at the time of writing. For example, the observance of the Law was connected with fruitfulness, peace and fullness of life, whereas non-observance was coupled with the opposite, which Scripture calls "death." We are told in Chapter Two and Three of Genesis that all this already was at the very beginning, but those chapters do not give us a concrete description of the forms—or the lack of form—in which man's dialogue with God actually took place. The story as given in Genesis neither denies nor confirms our conclusion that the first men of our species lived their religion in a manner that was adjusted to their primitive initial situation. It certainly does not enable us to imagine what that manner and form actually were.

Classical theologians will object: in any case, the account of Genesis tells us that the first men, chronologically speaking, the man of the first generation, sinned; in other words, they had already attained to a stage of development that enabled them to give a deliberate positive or negative reply to the offer of God's grace. We do not deny that such a reply was actually given.

In our turn, however, we ask: Does the account of genesis really tell us that sin was committed by the first parents of the human race? Does it really imply that we all descend from one human couple and that sin was committed by the first generation? Taking account of the whole of Scripture, we doubt that Genesis affirms those things. True, the chief personage of the Genesis chapters is characterized as the first individual man to whom we give the name "Adam"; he is thus singled out especially in the biblical genealogies, such as that of Chapter Five of Genesis. But within the story itself he is first of all man unqualified, "Everyman." And even when Adam, as in Romans, Chapter Five, is pictured as a historical figure, we notice nevertheless that the sins committed after him are taken jointly with his in contrast to Christ's redeeming obedience. There is also the fact that John does not mention the sin of Adam but only "the sin of the world," which is "taken away" by Christ.[33]

Is it perhaps permissible to connect the situation induced by original sin, not with the sin of one single individual, not with the first man in the chronological sense, but with the sin of the whole world? In such a case it might perhaps be of no importance exactly when and where sin entered the picture, and as a consequence, we could say that Revelation tells us nothing about the degree of self-consciousness and freedom of the first human generation.

When we limit ourselves to Scripture alone, it would seem that it gives us nothing more than the affirmation of the super-

---

[33] John 1, 29.

natural possibility of salvation for the first human beings, without any further detail. However, we must read Scripture within the framework of the Church and let our understanding of it be guided by authoritative teaching. The authority of the Church can tell us more than we get out of Scripture by our own exegesis. Taking this into account, it does seem that the Church's doctrinal authority draws more from the Bible than what we have gathered from the exegesis given above.

When we study the great declarations of the Council of Orange,[34] repeated and confirmed by the General Council of Trent,[35] we see that original sin, as affecting the children of mankind, is connected with the sin of Adam and him alone. This in itself does not exclude the sin of others, which brings us back to what we said a moment ago about the sin of the world. It remains difficult, nevertheless, not to attribute a separate proper influence to the first sin committed at a definite time by the first universal couple of parents, for the teaching Church connects with that sin the fact that the human nature we receive through generation has become subject to death, destined to a separation of body and soul, and that this was not the case before that sin had been committed.

Is it possible to by-pass that idea, which is especially affirmed in the first canon of the Council of Carthage?[36] Is it possible to interpret the entry of death into the world not as implying a change in man's nature but in his personal attitude toward death?

If this is possible, we are permitted to follow the interpretation we have delineated above. We can then refuse to worry about the precise time of the first sin and we do not have to affirm anything about the way the first human beings experienced their relation to God.

Even if we are obliged to admit that a sin was committed by those who were the first parents, chronologically speaking,

---

[34]Denzinger, nos. 101 ff.
[35]Denzinger, nos. 707-792.
[36]Denzinger, no. 101.

and that a state of immortality preceded that sin, we are not forced to postulate an explicit idea of God and salvation, for the refusal of love can also be made merely on the plane of human relations. Hence, in spite of everything, we can, at least along general lines, adhere to our first position that all we can say about the bestowing of grace upon the first human beings is that grace was given to them and that, on the other hand, that life of grace was lived in a primitive manner which is now beyond our conception.

This proposition, in its broad lines, applies also to the whole initial period that precedes the clear appearance of religiousness. We said already that we would like to extend this period till the beginning of the Neolithic Period with its characteristic agricultural civilizations. Some might object that there are traces pointing to human culture and religion before that time. This is undoubtedly true. We can almost say that one never finds any human remains without accompanying traces of man's attitude toward the mysteries of human life and death. On the other hand, aren't those traces very vague? Is it certain, for example, that the mutilated skulls of the Sinanthropus are indications of cannibalism? If so, is this a magic symptom? We see here corpses, and especially skulls, treated in a way that is alien to animals. Is this a sign of belief in personal immortality? Does it point to a cult of the dead? Again, we can point to the magic practices of paleolithic man, but do they signify religiousness and, if so, what kind of religiousness?

We believe that it is better to suspend judgment until the religion of paleolithic man is better known. Until then, it is better to keep our mind open to any possibility. That is why we also refrain from discussing the question whether the monotheism which we find in an unreflective form among the Pygmies, who in our own day represent the paleolithic type of culture, constitutes the original form of religion. We leave open the possibility that it was developed by way of a cult of ancestors, or that ancestor worship itself represents a form of decadence of monotheism, or even that the two kinds of religiousness are mutually independent. This is why we prefer not to use such ideas until the age is reached when man manifests his religion more clearly. To some extent we find such manifestations already in the Paleolithic Age among people who are hunters, and we certainly may not exclude the pastoral peoples which contributed to the origin of Israel. The most evident signs, however, are formed in the agricultural stages of development belonging to the Neolithic Age and the following periods.

RELIGIOUS SELF-EXPRESSION

With the Neolithic Age mankind entered upon a new youth. Its beginning, which goes back a few tens of thousands of years, still belongs to prehistorical times, for we possess no written records of it. Between 3000 and 2000 B.C., however, when documents make history possible, the neolithic culture is in bloom and fruitful, but that does not mean that it is really changed. Indeed we can say with Teilhard that up to our modern technological revolution we have not yet left the Neolithic Age, for this period continues to give us a model of human existence. It is within this Neolithic Age that the dialogue between us men and the God of our salvation, which began imperceptibly with humanity, becomes audible, that it is clearly expressed in Israel, and that it attains its fullness in the Incarnate Word.

In our own day, we are not only better able to approach the birth of the Noelithic Age on the basis of increasing archeological discoveries, but we also understand it better on account of our own experience of the present technological revolution. Technology gives man a more complete dominion over the world and, as a result, humanity develops, concentrates in cities, moves all over the globe; all men become neighbors and there are changes in regard to health, art, thinking, and our idea of God.

A similar revolution—though the process was much slower and less radical—must have taken place in human life when man began to put nature under his control through agriculture and cattle-raising. Whereas the man who lives on what can be obtained from hunting and the gathering of wild fruits is entirely dependent on nature, the man who cultivates the soil and raises stock adds his contribution to nature's seasonal operations. The multiplication of mankind led to this more intensive exploitation of natural resources and was in turn stimulated by that exploitation.

Men divided the earth among themselves. Agricultural people established themselves in fruitful river basins. Cattle-raisers moved from place to place as nomads or half-nomads. In the agriculture stage of culture, man attached himself to the soil. Villages and towns sprang up; there was an organized apportionment of land and irrigation of the soil. Social distinctions were formed, an apparatus of government appeared, and as early as 2500 years B.C. Egypt already had a bureaucracy. Technology and the diversification of labor gave opportunities for the development of culture. Art and writing made it possible to know ancient humanity in a direct way. All this attained to a full flowering in the great empires that were established in the fruitful valleys of China, India, Mesopotamia, and Egypt.

It is between the last two of these empires that Israel's history unfolded. Israel's history is insignificant from the political standpoint, but this group of people is interesting even from the human standpoint, for its history comprises all the human situations with respect to the earth that are possible in the Neolithic Age. The Hebrews are half-nomads, they settle down as Israelites, become farmers who live in villages and towns, they build a kingdom and again lose everything in exile. They experience everything that neolithic man can meet with and undergo: they roam, they settle down, they know slavery and independence, they live together and are dispersed. That is why the periods of their history can serve even today as an illustration for our own situations.

In regard to neolithic man, it is no longer necessary to arrive by way of conclusion at the fact that he possessed an inner life such as we have. We are able to recognize him as being in every respect like ourselves. This we see already in his houses, his tools, his works of art. It becomes even more evident when he has left literature behind, in which we see him in his love and his hatred, and also in his religion. In that way, the conclusions we drew on the basis of our faith in God's universal will of salvation from the beginning of mankind, now are confirmed by signs. In the Neolithic Age, we see and hear man's acceptance or rejection of God's invitation to salvation. Man finds God in creation, in the seasons which he sanctifies by feasts, in sacred places on mountains and near springs. The dialogue between God and man expresses itself particularly at the stage of agricultural civilization. God is honored as He who renews everything in springtime. He is appealed to as He who grants fruitfulness. He is thanked for the harvest.

When man begins to live in houses, he recognizes God's presence in temples. Sometimes towns or tribes assemble around sanctuaries. It is possible that the twelve tribes of Israel formed originally such a kind of "amphictyony." Within the temples, God's presence is more definitely expressed in shrines or images, sacrifices are offered, hymns are sung, and prayers said. Together with the organization of daily life, there is the organization of religion: a priesthood arises, the king himself is closely connected with worship, he is even related to the divinity. The whole of life, which we now call civil, is permeated with religion.

When we look at those religious manifestations from the standpoint of the Old Testament, we see them, as it were, over the wall that separates Israel from the Gentiles. With very few exceptions—which practically all refer to the distant past or to the messianic future—they are described as not-the-people-of-God, their religion is idolatry, their gods are falsehood and shame. However, let us stress that that view was also a divine judgment upon them and that the biblical characterizations of those religions were true. That is why we will repeat them, but we must add the remark that the Old Testament does not present a complete image of reality.

Basing ourselves upon some texts of the New Testament which we have already mentioned, but especially upon the fact that Christ has broken down the wall of separation, we may also say that God was already at work in the hearts of the pagans, and hence also in their religiousness, to prepare the way for His only-begotten Son. Looking at it more closely, we see that the pagan religiousness, purified and re-formed, of course, was taken over by Israel itself and in this way contributed to make Christ's message more plain to us.

Christ, while changing everything, took over the Old Testament, and the Old Testament did the same with the religious forms found in its surroundings. Hence Christ's word that He had "not come to destroy but to fulfill"[37] applies not only to the Old Covenant, but also, in a broader sense, to God's dialogue with other peoples and the forms they give to this dialogue. For this reason, the Old Testament is still the preparatory school and the dictionary which enable us to understand the Revelation given in Christ, but man's universal religiousness is the dictionary that gives us an understanding of the Old Testament.

If the social life of mankind had not been pervaded with worship, a priesthood, temple, sacrifices, blessings, prayers, feasts, sacred traditions and sacred writings, we would not possess the apparatus of concepts, words and signs and rites through which we now can meet Christ. If we abstract from and discard the forms of religiosity developed since the Neolithic Age, we can hardly imagine what words and signs the Son of God could have used to meet and contact us as our fellow-man. We do not want to claim that no other means would have been possible for God, but we must affirm that in fact He has not done it in another way. This goes to show the priceless positive value of the religious culture that was developed by mankind. Only after saying this, can we point out the dark side of this religious culture to the extent that it was not incorporated in Israel and in Christ, but remained "pagan."

---

[37]Matt. 5, 17.

The dark side, or rather the real dangers which pagan religiousness had for the faith of Israel and for the faith of everyone, can be reduced to two words: idolatry and an empty formalism of worship. Most notable is Israel's battle against idolatry. Here we are in the presence of a consent to the original temptation: "you shall be as gods"[38] by your own powers. Man lays hold of the divine itself. He wants to have the divinity at his disposal. The mere fact that a tribe or a city speaks of "its own" god is not necessarily an expression of that tendency, but such an expression is present as soon as they recognize gods of other human groups as equivalent to their own, and especially when the operations of nature are divided among gods; for example, when a god or goddess of the earth is honored alongside a god of heaven. People belonging to agricultural civilizations were strongly inclined to such a division. Likewise, the mere fact that one's God is venerated under an image does not constitute idolatry, but rather the fact that the divinity is seized and brought down to the level of man. In other words, idolatry is the veneration of images coupled with the intentions we have described.

We need not enter into detail regarding the fierce battle of the prophets of Israel against the ever-threatening danger of idolatry. Practically throughout the Old Testament— with some sort of exception in chapter fourteen of Wisdom[39] —that controversy is conducted in a very primitive way. The powerlessness of the material image is simply transferred to the god who is represented by it: "They have feet and walk not," etc.[40]

Before condemning that kind of argumentation, we should realize how fearful and powerful the gods, especially those of the great neighboring nations, appeared to Israel, and how greatly those who worshipped those statues identified

---

[38]Gen. 3, 5.

[39]"In the process of time . . . statues were worshipped by the commandment of tyrants . . . , the multitude of men, carried away by the beauty of the work, took him now for a god that a little before was but honored as a man." Wis. 14, 8-31.

[40]Ps. 115, 4-7; Is. 44; Baruch 6.

them with their gods. In any case, the prophets do not teach us to condemn representations of God, but they condemn the false ideas about God, and man's attempt to control the divine. Israel saw this false fundamental attitude imbedded in the polytheistic worship of images.

The same attitude was present also in more primitive religions or was absorbed into higher and more universal forms, such as the official religion of the Romans and that of the Hindus. Moreover, the same attitude is also present in more abstract tendencies of pantheistic religions, particularly those found in Asia. The divine condemnation uttered by the prophets of Israel remains valid when we consider ancient and new religions theologically. Yet it must be granted that the interpretation of religious expressions remains a very delicate task.

The judgment of the prophets transcended all nationalist prejudice, as we can see by the fact that they did not spare the particular worship of Yahweh as practiced by their own people. In this respect, they warned against the second danger that had arisen since the beginning of the Neolithic Age, that of empty formalism and magic. Man adopts certain forms in his dialogue with God and these enable him to express his dialogue, but he is tempted to forget the fact that this dialogue encompasses the whole of human life without any exception. God bestows favors and graces upon our whole existence. Our whole life must be our answer, expressed in surrender, service and love.

The distinct world of worship, however, is always a temptation for sinful man to confine himself to that in his relations with God. That is why the prophets scourge a religiousness which is restricted to the Temple and the Sabbath. Their denunciations are sometimes so vehement that they seem to condemn the whole Temple worship, whereas they are merely condemning wrong attitudes.[41] These attitudes consist either in evading other duties, such as those of charity toward the

---

[41]Cf. for example, Amos 5, 21-27; Osee 6, 6; Is. 1, 11-17; Jer. 7; Ps. 49.

neighbor and justice, or in the use of magic means to secure God's presence, and reliance on one's own sacrifices to force God to protect His people. Because the prophets discerned the weak aspects and the dangers of the whole world of religious signs and symbols, they also had no difficulty in realizing the relativity of that world.

There is nothing definitive in that world according to the mind of the prophets. Jeremia,[42] already lets the ark disappear in the messianic economy of salvation. Zacharia[43] sees everything as being as holy as the Temple, and in the new Jerusalem of St. John's Apocalypse[44] there is no Temple any more. That view is accompanied by the insight that even now the world of religious expression can be simplified, because man's "heart" is the proper place where he should express his reply to God's offer of salvation. This discernment of the value of simplification of forms of worship is present sometimes even in pagan religions. However, these equally favor a multiplication of signs and the use of magic that strangles the faith, whereas signs and symbols should be means to enlighten faith.

In this way, we view pagan religiousness as a struggle. Men's genuine answer to the God of salvation takes shape in a world of signs, but at the same time idolatry, polytheism and pantheism, empty formalism, and magic religious practices add to this answer the expression of proud rejection or usurpation of God's grace. Grace and sin live side by side in those religions. Hence we are permitted to have a genuine admiration for the words and images that are found in non-Christian religions, as they are offered to us, for example, in the book, *The World's Great Religions.*[45] We

---

[42]"They shall say no more: The ark of the covenant . . . neither shall it be visited, neither shall that be done any more." Jer. 3, 16.

[43]"In that day . . . every caldron in Jerusalem and Juda shall be sanctified to the Lord of hosts." Zach. 14, 20.

[44]"I saw no temple therein, for the Lord God almighty and the Lamb are the temple thereof." Apoc. 21, 22.

[45]New York, 1957. Illustrated articles on Hinduism, Buddhism, the Philosophy of China, Islam, Judaism, Christianity. For a theological evaluation of non-Christian religions, see Karl Rahner, "Das Christentum und die nichtchristlichen Religionen," vol. IV of *Schriften zur Theologie.*

may rejoice with a Christian heart in such manifestations. It would be naive, however, not to temper this admiration by noting also the dark side and the shadows in them— which we so readily note in our own Christian way of life. The struggle continues within those religions. The transition from them to Christianity will be at the same time an ascent to Him who "came to fulfill" all things and a conversion from the service of idols "to serving the living and true God."[46] This conversion we must now consider in Israel. In this people, God, by His initiatives so full of grace, brought clarity to the confused struggle of paganism, and converted human hearts to Himself.

CLARITY IN ISRAEL

As we have seen, it is not possible to determine exactly the beginning of the second phase in the history of salvation. There is a similar difficulty with respect to the third phase. The origin of the chosen people is situated somewhere in the period of transition from the nomadic life of the pastoral tribes to their settled and agricultural life in Canaan. Before their entry and settlement in Canaan, the patriarchal clan wandered about and dwelt in Egypt and near Sinai. It has been doubted on historical grounds that the two series of adventures were shared in common by the twelve tribes.

One thing, however, they had in common, a thing inherited from their ancestors: faith in the one Yahweh, the God of salvation. This faith had such a hold on that people that they passed from henotheism to strict monotheism and thus overcame the persistent polytheistic temptation of the country in which they had settled down.

As we remarked already, this monotheism is the only new element in the religiousness of Israel, but it is an element that renovates everything. Sporadic efforts of similar purification occurred in other religions and, con-

---

[46] 1 Thes. 1, 9.

versely, the Israelites sinned frequently and seriously by idolatry. However, Israel was unique because its faith in the one true God managed to maintain itself in the superior civilization of Canaan. This faith was victorious in the prophets. In the end it insured the continued existence of the Jews as a people during and after the Babylonian Captivity, in spite of the numerous political and cultural factors that threatened its existence.

It is this monotheistic faith that gave Israel its own proper character. Its worship was greatly enriched when the half-nomadic Hebrews became settled farmers in Canaan. Yahweh now came to live in temples and, from being the God of Sinai, He became the God of Sion. The feast of the first lambs became the feast of unleavened breads. Sacrifices and the priesthood were organized and regulated by an elaborate liturgical law. A kingdom was formed. But monotheism did more than hold its own against the temptations inherent in the cultural and liturgical elements which the Israelites borrowed from their neighbors. It put its stamp on the forms of worship it had taken over. It purified and clarified them. It forbade images and statues and finally had only one temple. The king was the anointed of Yahweh, but was deprived of a semi-divine power over law and worship.

In the end, Israel was expelled from its soil and robbed of everything in which its faith had become incarnate. However, God's personal presence then took the place of the Temple made by hands, and the memory of the kings served as material for prophecies concerning the future anointed. As a result of this "disincarnation," Israel's religion became more interior and profound, a process which had been at work previously in the prophets.

Israel stood before the God of its Covenant like other peoples, but on account of its faith in the one, transcendent God, it realized that the alliance was not based on a mutual agreement but on God's election, and that the Covenant remained not by natural contributions, but in virtue of Yahweh's merciful fidelity. The Covenant was seen fundamentally as

God's will, God's "testament." Worship had value only when accompanied by the service of the Lord, bridal fidelity to Yahweh, faith and the expectation of the "poor of Yahweh." Man himself is personalized as he stands before the "living," that is, the personal God, Yahweh. For this reason "the heart" has always precedence over public worship and the observance of legal prescriptions.

Likewise, God's action in those who are His own, and His great deeds for His people, transcend His operation in nature: the feast of the lambs and the breads becomes the feast of Exodus, the God of the seasons becomes the God of salvation and final fulfillment, the recurrence of nature's events is replaced by the memory of the great deeds of Yahweh and the expectation of His Day. When Yahweh becomes a God of history, man also takes his place in it and becomes responsible for his own earthly life. Yahweh appears as Judge as well as Savior. Man's greatest want is seen to be rooted in sin. God's salvation and fulfillment is a liberation from sin, and the acceptance of salvation requires conversion.

This summary shows to some extent that the chosen people did not have a uniform religiousness throughout their existence. They had a true history that was full of development and struggle. This history unfolded in two phases: the phase of an ever stronger establishment and possession, and the phase of exile and spiritualization. Within that history, we see all the situations of our human existence since the beginning of the Neolithic Age: that of nomads, of settlers in villages and towns, of the enslaved and the exiled. That is why the Bible, particularly the Old Testament, is so universally human and opens the way to God in so many different situations of human existence.

The people of the Old Covenant, living as they did within those diverse situations of earthly existence, passed through stages of progress and decline in their union with God, so that their history is at the same time a sort of prefiguration of the Church history of later years within a definite culture. We shall revert to this point later. Let us now underline

95

the majestic development which God wrought within those situations. When we study the literary genres and the historical circumstances, we are not inclined to conceive "the great works of God" in the spectacular way in which they are described in the sacred writings, particularly those of the cycle of the exodus and the entry into Canaan. What causes our admiration throughout is the miracle of Israel, the miracle of Yahweh, who as the one true and living God so perfectly conquered the heart of the people that it not only kept its faith in Him, but made this faith the very driving force enabling it to rise over and over again.

Seen against the background of the pagan religions, that permanence of monotheism is a great historical miracle, for the development of pagan religions often spells the ruin of a pure approach to God in favor of polytheism and pantheism. And if monotheism reappears in those pagan religions, it is too weak to cure the generality of the people of the decadent forms of religion which it has absorbed.

Looking at it more closely, we can mention here the twice repeated miracle of the victory of Israel's monotheistic faith in its contact with a polytheistic culture that was superior to its own; namely, with that of the Canaanites and those of the great empires, from that of Babylon to that of Rome. This miracle, moreover, was not accomplished by a wave of the wand, but God's grace engaged in a severe struggle and won a victory against powerful incarnations of human refusal and abuse of God's grace. Those who constituted the core of Israel were always engaged in battle: the prophets, the Macchabean fighters and martyrs, and finally the "poor of Yahweh" had to fight against a practice of worship and an observance of the Law that had degenerated into a sort of magic. They were always weak, but they always conquered through their faith, that is, by the power of God. They thus foreshadowed a new struggle—that of Christ, who brought the fullness of God's salvation, against the flood of wickedness that carried Him to His crucifixion.

THE FULLNESS IN CHRIST

The dialogue between God and man is audible throughout the Neolithic Age, but it rings clear only in the religion of the Jews, "from whom is the Christ according to the flesh, who is over all things, God blessed forever."[47] After God has brought this dialogue to clarity in Israel, where "at sundry times and in divers manners He spoke in time past to the fathers by the prophets," He now "in these days has spoken to us by his Son."[48]

God now directs to us the Word who was eternally with Him and is like to Him and, together with His Word, He also gives us His eternal and personal Spirit of Love. When the manifestation of God in all His transcendence attains its fullness—at least for the remnant whom He had chosen— God then shows and gives Himself entirely as He is: He becomes our Father through His Only-begotten, who is our fellow-man, and both give us the Divine Spirit.

Just as the only thing that was new in Israel was its monotheism, which at the same time renewed everything, so is it with Christ in the New Testament. Forms and words and concepts had already been fashioned. That is why the text of the Old Testament is four times as extensive as that of the New. But now everything becomes new; nothing is abolished, but everything is completed, though Christ breaks it open, as "new wine breaks old skins." "By coming Himself," says St. Irenaeus, "He has brought all newness."

Christ is the perfect Mediator. Hence He is at the same time Temple, Image, and Priest. He is the supreme King and final Judge as well as the Norm of all. The New Israel, which is the Church of all peoples, is established on Him. The ritualistic worship is replaced by signs which make present and apply His Sacrifice. The Law is absorbed in the Spirit, and the Covenant is eternal, for it is made unbreakable by Him.

---

[47]Rom. 9, 5.
[48]Hebr. 1, 1.

In this way, the spheres of the recognition of God in nature and in history are taken up in the encounter with God in Christ and His salvific deeds. The Jewish Passover becomes the feast of Christ's death and resurrection. Thus Christianity comes down to belonging to, and being in, Christ, and we shall finally be judged according to our attitude toward Christ. With Him, therefore, the preparatory stage of all peoples and also of Israel has come to an end, for we now live in "the fullness of time,"[49] even in "the last days."[50]

In Israel, God's dialogue with man constantly had to struggle in order to obtain a hearing and to become more manifest. It was inevitable that a similar struggle would occur when God desired to impart His fullness in Christ. In fact, the Lord's wrestling with man reached its apex at the beginning of the Christian era. During Christ's earthly life, the sin of the world reaches its high mark in man's rejection of Him by what Guardini calls "the second Fall."[51] At the same time, Christ's victory is definitive and "now will the prince of the world be cast out."[52] The Christ who had been rejected conquers as risen, by giving us a share in His Spirit. The victory remains assured in His Church by the fact that His message and the signs of salvation do not lose their force through the sinfulness of His human ministers. However, this idea implies at the same time that a fierce struggle will continue even in the fullness of time.

In other words, history goes on even in this fullness, and there is still a history of salvation. True, Revelation and the work of salvation are completed with Christ, so that He is "the Last,"[53] "the last Adam,"[54] and through Him we live in "the last days,"[55] even in "the last hour."[56] The reason is that in the Man who is His own Son, God has spoken most

---

[49]Gal. 4, 4.
[50]Heb. 1, 2.
[51]Romano Guardini, *The Lord,* Chicago, 1954, p. 98.
[52]John 12, 31.
[53]Apoc. 1, 17; 2, 8; 22, 13.
[54]1 Cor. 15, 45.
[55]Tim. 3, 1; 2 Pet. 3, 3.
[56]1 John 2, 18.

fully and has come to us. Thus mankind has entered into the highest and most profound form of communion with God. Nevertheless, this eternal Son of God is also truly and fully man. Consequently, He will make history with us and we with Him. That is why, as man, He not only grew in age but also "in wisdom and grace before God and men."[57] It was principally for that reason that He desired to enter into our history and existence, and in order that we could be taken up into His own life, He in us and we in Him.

Since the coming of Christ, there is still a further development of what is human, a development of which we are today discovering unsuspected dimensions. This constructive development is significant for salvation, and this applies even to today's industrial revolution. Besides, there is a progress in the history of salvation that is woven into human history. We could describe this progress of the history of salvation through man's entrance into Christ's fullness, by saying that there is still an "Old Testament"[58] expectation within this fullness, there is still an ascent toward Christ who has already come, as the Church reminds us in her annual celebration of Advent.

Of course, this statement, is true of mankind as a whole, first of all, for in great part it is still on its way to this fullness. It is also true of the Church itself. Although the fullness is fundamentally and inviolably established in her, this fullness can receive an ever more perfect unfolding. Let us begin with the latter point.

In spite of the fact that the Spirit of Christ guarantees the Church's fidelity to the profession of faith and the sacraments, she remains the holy Church of sinners. Expressing it more universally, she is the fullness of the times in those who are still in the process of growth, she is the fatherland in which we are still on our way as pilgrims. We Christians of all countries and times should advance toward the salvation that is given us in Christ. In reality, however, we often stray

---

[57]Luke 2, 52.
[58]Hebr. 5, 8 ff.

away from it, but we return hopefully again, attracted by grace. The Church makes gains, suffers losses, regains ground in various countries and human communities, and she is principally called to penetrate ever more deeply into our human life, sanctifying and completing it.

Within a particular civilization, one can recognize the two movements which we have distinguished in the people of God in the Old Testament. First, through the entrance of the Church into this world of culture, there is embodiment of the Christian faith into the elements of this culture. Then there is the loss of those borrowed forms, when that culture for some reason becomes lost to the Church. Echoes of this movement of "embodiment" and adoption of the Canaanite forms of worship into the Hebrew religion can be discerned in the greater development and organization of worship and religion that began with the religious peace granted by Constantine in the time of the Church Fathers. The same thing occurs also in countries where the Church, through her missionaries, absorbs a certain culture and expresses herself in its forms.

There is an outstanding example of this embodiment in the European Middle Ages. The Church became intimately connected with the forms of culture which she found in the Germanic peoples and with others she had borrowed from Roman antiquity and passed on to those peoples. Thus, she adopted the form of the social structure of the time—to such an extent that even today Church functions continue to retain the character of positions in society. In reverse, she strongly sacralized and clericalized that society.

In our own time, we witness a contrary movement. The Church sheds her medieval embodiment, not only in order to prepare for her "incarnation" in cultures outside Europe and America, but also because western man himself no longer lives in those antiquated forms. Western man, engaged as he is in technological revolution, is leaving the Neolithic Age. He moves away from the agricultural mode of life toward that dictated by industry, and with this transition come new images of man, the world, and God. From this change there result, for example, the decrease of external forms in favor of sacramental communion with the Lord, the finding of God, above and outside all liturgical and clerical forms, in the whole of God's creation.

Here, then, is something like what happened at the time of the prophets, the spiritualization of the Old Testament during and after the Babylonian Captivity. However, it is done now in a much more radical way, for the Jewish sense of security in the Law or the restoration of the ancient Temple are no longer the ideal to be striven for. In their stead, there is rather the faithful expectation of the "poor of Yahweh."

In this movement, western culture itself breaks down its walls of separation. All peoples meet intensively and often profoundly, although there are also frequent conflicts. The Church now has means at her disposal for a more intense and profound encounter with mankind outside its frontiers than was possible in former times. Those peoples come in greater numbers to "Christian" countries. They are able to meet the Church. Conversely, the Church, being freed from the colonizing West, can enter into the "heart" of those populations, instead of having only a peripheral contact as was the case until recently.

If those possibilites are to be realized, we must first learn to know those peoples and particularly their forms of religiousness. In this respect it is important to recall what we have said about the second phase of the general history of salvation, for precisely this phase has continued to exist in them. We must appreciate the non-Christian religions as pre-Christian. This means that we must recognize their value for what they contain and express in God's dialogue with man. At the same time, however, we must also repeat the protest of the prophets against the human usurpation and man's refusal that may be found in those religions. The pre-Christian religions fulfill their role in the general history of salvation, as long as Christianity has not penetrated into their territory. What ultimately determines the place of a certain human community in the history of salvation is not the fact of Christ's coming into the whole world by His incarnation and glorification, but His coming into that people through His missionaries in a way that constitutes a true encounter of the core of that people with the core of Christ's Church. What we may be permitted to call "the old testament of the pagans," in virtue of what we have said above, loses its validity when it actually encounters the New Testament in Christ. The human community in question is then faced, as Guardini remarks, with the choice of John the Baptist: to become smaller as a precursor in the presence of the Greater, or to prefer and assert itself and reject the Savior.

The non-Christian religions continue to exist in their "old testament times" as long as the encounter with Christ has not taken place in virtue of the Church's missionary activity. Nevertheless, the existence of the Church, as she is established already on the earth, and even the existence of Israel, cannot be without influence. In regard to the latter, the Jewish diaspora exercised a profound influence at the beginning of our era, certainly in the milieu of proselytes and God-fearing people, but also outside those circles.

Much more extensive is the later influence of Islam, which in a sense also goes back to Israel's faith in God. Islam replaced polytheism by a most strict monotheism in large sections of Asia and Africa. We are justified in looking upon it as an offshoot of Jewish monotheism. At first sight, it seems harshly theocratic and legalistic, but it also points to Allah "the compassionate and merciful" and even directs attention to the "Prophet Jesus." These ideas have nourished the piety of Mohammedan mystics and they have died for them. For that reason, we can call Islam a very distant offshoot of Christianity itself, which has spread over the world. Also offsprings of Christianity, in a stricter sense, are the Christian heresies which have engaged in missionary activity; e.g., Nestorianism, a sect which spread as far as Japan.

Are we also permitted to suppose that there are completely hidden forces at work, besides those historically ascertainable influences that proceed from Christianity? Such a possibility is certainly not to be excluded, if we recognize the power of prayer. Some may see Christ at work in the more profound forms of religiousness of Hinduism and Buddhism, the bhakti piety, and in man's redeeming charity toward his fellow-men.[59] It is possible that God's pre-Christian work of salvation fashioned those high forms, just as it led Jewish piety to the faith and the surrender of the "poor of Yahweh."

In all that we have said until now, we have constantly interpreted the religions that exist outside of Christianity as *pre*-Christian. There still remains a very serious problem, specifically for our western world of culture. Are we not in the presence of a multitude of currents that can only be called *post*-Christian, and which, in part, also consider themselves as such? This is undeniably true. To the extent that it broke away from the Church of Christ, the Reformation may be called the beginning of those currents, but there are far more compelling reasons to call *post*-Christian those currents that simply broke away from Christianity and even turned their back to religion.

Still, if we take God's universal salvific will seriously, even in those currents there must be present fundamentally a way that leads to Christ's fullness. It is, of course, a more difficult way, but it might perhaps lead to a fuller possession of that fullness. As regards the Reformation, we must say that it is a prophetism but also, unfortunately, a schism. At the same time, if those whom we call Reformed Christians were to recognize the full profession of faith and the sacramental system of the Church of Rome, they would bring with them great promises of personal and scriptural reflection and so also they would open possibilities for a richer and fuller life of the Church. Can we say likewise that, if Marxists and humanists discovered Christ, they also would make Christians recognize better Christ's countenance in

---

[59]Regarding Islam, Hinduism and Buddhism, see the article of J. H. Walgrave, "De heilshistorische verhouding tussen de Kerk en de niet-christelijke godsdiensten," *Tijdschrift voor Theologie*, Vol. 1 (1961), pp. 148-169.

their fellow-men? When we reflect on God's will of salvation, we are prompted to reply here also in the affirmative.

What exists outside the pale of Christianity is pre-Christian and hence is on the way. He who says that the men who are outside the frontiers of the Church can also be saved and that, therefore, we should not inflict our preaching on them, misjudges one actual element in their situation with respect to salvation. God speaks to them at the stage they have reached in the history of mankind. He speaks to them on the road they follow. Hence they have the obligation, to the extent they are aware of it, of going to the end of the road on which they are. This means, therefore, that the Church must go to them and that the Lord's command of making all men His disciples[60] retains its full force and validity.

When we look at missionary work in the light of our present consideration, it still remains a duty of the Church, but we realize also the more profound truth that this work is not a one-sided endeavor but an encounter, and it is this not merely on the human plane but on the plane of God's salvific work itself. For the same God who sends us to preach His only-begotten Son, is already at work preparing the way for Him. His Spirit sends messengers from here, and over there He calls men to the fullness of Christ.

All these movements—that which goes toward Christ's Church, that which goes out from her, and certainly that which exists within her—never reach completion on this earth, for our whole earthly existence is history. That is why the universal history of salvation in all its parts tends to the "eschaton," the last end or the beginning of what will be definitive. The things we are to expect at that time are already pictured at the end of the Old Testament. Then shall take place the definitive encounter of the whole man with the God of his salvation, hence resurrection, judgment, and full redemption.

---

[60]"Go, therefore, and make disciples of all nations." Matt. 28, 19.

The New Testament does not really add anything new to this picture, except the unique newness of Christ. Because the encounter with God reached its fullness in Him, the day of Yahweh necessarily becomes the day of Christ, the day on which we shall rise with our bodies as the expression of the response to Him which we fashioned during our whole earthly life. Then also will evolution and history come to an end, for the Son of God will have attained fullness as our fellow-man and we attain fullness as His fellow-men.

Evolution and history had their stages of gradual development, but also their explosive forward leaps. The great leap of "hominization" was followed on the human level by great cultural changes, such as the birth of the Neolithic Age and probably also the technological revolution of our own day.

The supernatural contact between God and man has always been present in the history of salvation, but within it there occurred also the mighty leaps of Israel's vocation and the incarnation and glorification of God's Son. The Last Day will give us the greatest leap of all on the human level, for we shall then leave evolution and history behind and enter into the definitive state of eternity. This, at the same time, will be a leap in the history of salvation by which the conquering presence of the Son of God finally will win complete victory and be fully revealed. No veil or struggle will any longer put an obstacle in the way of those who are loyal to Him, for through His Incarnate Word God will then "be all in all."[61]

---

[61] 1 Cor. 15, 28.

CHAPTER FOUR

MARRIAGE IN THE PERSPECTIVE OF THE HISTORY OF SALVATION

Human existence makes history. There are no aspects of our human existence that did not slowly develop to their present condition. Man has gained an ever greater dominion over the earth, as fruit-gatherer, hunter, cattle-breeder, husbandman, and industrialist. The common bond between men has also grown increasingly closer, as well as more personal and more profound. Mankind has progressed from tribal unions to a world union of states, from slavery to a society of cooperative labor, from the patriarchal sib to the democratic type of family.

Man's attitude toward God underwent a similar development. Man seeks God first on the heights or in temples built amidst human dwellings. He fashions forms of worship and constructs mythologies. More important than this is that God allows Himself to be found progressively in greater depth and grandeur. He wills that all men should be saved and should come to the knowledge of the truth. On the long road towards that goal, He is with man, imparting His grace, in the paradise of the first encounter, but also again and again since sin entered the world. The time before Abraham is not a vacuum, for a history of salvation and perdition is already developing. There is a confused dialogue between God and man, followed by the clearness which God sheds in Israel, before His eternal Word comes and speaks in our human existence.

Within that history, we find marriage. In the story of creation, as given in the first chapter of Genesis, the condition of man versus woman and the multiplication of mankind are connected with man's dominion over the earth and with God's plan. The relations to the earth, to fellow-men and

106

God always touch one another and are particularly intertwined in marriage. The division of labor in primitive human society determines at the same time the character of the family from the standpoint of the rights of father and mother. Today we witness a similar change in family relations, particularly those between husband and wife, because one or both work outside the family circle. Because modern culture gathers in cities, there is a particularly urgent question regarding the relationship between the purposes of marriage.

However, the primary factor that most profoundly influences marriage is the extent to which human beings look upon and accept one another as persons—in particular, the extent to which man and woman accept each other as persons. Man's attitude toward his fellow-man, in its turn, is profoundly affected by, and reciprocal to, man's attitude toward God. This relationship is not surprising, since the second commandment is like to the first. In marriage, man experiences the nearness of God as Creator and a reflection of the communion with God which He offers to men. That is why Leo XIII, in his encyclical *Arcanum,* tells us that all married life is sacred. For this reason, we shall be able to study the high points of the history of marriage, if we determine its place in the history of salvation of mankind, which history, as we have seen, has its high points in the history of Israel and the history of the Church.

MONOGAMY

For us Christians, and even for western man in general, marriage is monogamous. It is the union of one man and one woman. The monogamous character of marriage developed in many places and eras. Added to that, within the Judaeo-Christian Revelation, man came to realize that monogamous marriage is rooted in the nature of man and hence is based on God's own creative will.

However, in this matter also there was a gradual development. In fact, the starting point in Israel lies at a fairly low level. It is lower, for instance, than that of the ancient Babylonian law as contained in the Code of Hammurabi, for the latter permits concubinage only as subordinate to the principle that marriage is monogamous. So also, divorce was unknown in Egypt. On the contrary, the patriarchs of Israel and also the men who belonged to the earlier period of the kings had more than one wife in the proper sense of this term. Polygamy was assumed to be the normal thing in the Mosaic Law.[1]

On the other hand, in the more recent literature of the Sapiential books, when the good woman is praised and the bad one is censured, we notice a different background. Here there is always the union of one woman with one man: "He who takes a wife acquires a precious good, a help similar to himself, a column of support."[2] "A friend and companion give their counsel in season, but above them both is an intelligent wife."[3]

We can imagine also that the story about the earthly paradise, to which one of these texts alludes, exercised an influence upon the growth of the practice and appreciation of monogamy. For, in that account, the woman, in contrast to the animals, is the helpmate who is like to the man and his only partner in human existence: "they shall be two in one flesh."[4]

The definitive step toward monogamy, however, is taken only in the New Testament in a pronouncement of Christ Himself. It is true that Judaism in His time, like the Greco-Roman world, had practically abolished simultaneous polygamy, but the repudiation of one's wife was commonly accepted. The only point of debate among the Jews was whether a man could repudiate his wife only for grave reasons or "for any cause,"[5] as was claimed by lax casuists.

---

[1]Ex. 21, 10; Lev. 18, 17 ff; Deut. 21, 15-17.
[2]Eccli. 36, 24.
[3]Eccli. 40, 23.
[4]Gen. 2, 24.
[5]Matt. 19, 3.

When the lax interpretation was put before Christ, He rejected it. This does not mean that He approved a divorce for grave motives. On the contrary, he affirmed the complete indissolubility of marriage. We find this declaration in St. Mark,[6] twice in St. Matthew,[7] and in St. Luke.[8] St. Paul later reflected upon it, saying: "But to those who are married, not I, but the Lord commands that a wife is not to depart from her husband, and if she departs, that she is to remain unmarried or be reconciled to her husband. And let not a husband put away his wife."[9] Before that the Apostle had determined the rights of both in married life: "The wife has not authority over her body, but the husband; the husband likewise had not authority over his body, but the wife."[10] Man and woman have given themselves as equals to one another for life: such is marriage since Christ.

The description which Chapter Ten of St. Mark and Chapter Nineteen of St. Matthew give of Christ's conversation with the Pharisees and His disciples impress us as faithfully reporting something that happened. Nevertheless, the inspired writers did not have for their primary intention to give a literal transcription of Christ's actual words. They rather transmitted them according to the Lord's intention in terms that were important for the situation of the Church at the time of writing. That is why Luke, and also Matthew in his first account,[11] put Christ's pronouncement regarding the indissolubility of marriage in a different context. St. Paul, who addressed himself to those who were living in the loose society of Corinth, does not speak about the repudiation of the woman by the man, but about the running away of the woman herself.

We become expecially aware of the *"Sitz im Leben"* and the concrete circumstances of the Church, by what is added

---

[6]Mark 10, 2-12.
[7]Matt. 4, 31 f.; 19, 3-10.
[8]Luke 16, 16.
[9]1 Cor. 7, 10 ff.
[10]1 Cor. 7, 4.
[11]Matt. 5, 31, f.

by St. Matthew alone.[12]   This addition, at first sight, seems
to restrict the absolute pronouncement which Christ gives
elsewhere; it states: "except for immorality."   Saint
Matthew's Gospel is addressed to Christian converts from
Judaism and shows a particular interest in the fulfillment
of the Law in the New Testament.[13]   The Jewish Law
forbade marriage within certain degrees of relationship,[14]
a practice that was not uncommon among neighboring pagan
nations.   The Jews looked upon marriages within forbidden
degrees as illegitimate unions, as concubinage, as immorality.
The Christian converts from Judaism thought likewise.
That is why St. James proposed at the Council of the Apostles
that the converts from paganism should be dispensed from
the whole Jewish Law except the abstention from a few
things, such as "immorality."[15]

It seems most probable that Matthew has this "immorality"
in mind in that clause which is found only in his Gospel
as an addition to Christ's pronouncement.   In that case,
the clause means that indissolubility does not apply to a
union that is not a marriage but rather "immorality."   Seen
in this light, the clause is a closer determination of what
is to be understood by "marriage."   It does not establish
an exception to the law of indissolubility.

Moreover, it is most unlikely that Our Lord would have
made such an exception, for St. Paul conceives Christ's
prohibition as absolute, and both St. Mark and St. Luke
report Christ's declaration without any reservation on His
part.   Again, even in St. Matthew we are told that Christ's
disciples thought that His declaration was severe: "If the
case of a man with his wife is so, it is not expedient to
marry."[16]

In any case, the eastern separated churches and Protes-
tantism cannot appeal to that text if they wish to justify their

---

[12]Matt. 5, 32; 19, 9.
[13]Matt. 5, 17-19.
[14]Lev. 18, 6-18.
[15]Acts 15, 20.
[16]Matt. 19, 10.

contention that divorce is permissible for *adultery,* for the Bible distinguishes "immorality" from "adultery", and the term "adultery" does not appear in that text of Matthew.

All this does not mean, however, that the clause given by St. Matthew has only an antiquarian interest for us. It shows us, on the contrary, that the Church, when she proclaims Christ's law about marriage, has the duty to declare what marriage is and what it is not. This applies not only to cases of marriage within the forbidden degrees, but also to unions that are contracted without the freedom and the knowledge which in a particular cultural situation are required for marriage.

We saw already that the writer of the story of Eden places the institution of marriage at the beginning of mankind and that he depicts it as monogamous.[17] In St. Mark[18] and St. Matthew, Christ refers to that text and He makes it even more explicit, for instead of "they" He says "the two" and connects it with the words of Genesis 1, 27, concerning the creation of the two sexes: "Have you not read that the Creator, from the beginning, made them male and female and said: 'For this cause a man shall leave his father and mother, and cleave to his wife, and the two shall become one flesh'? Therefore now they are no longer two, but one flesh. What therefore God has joined together, let no man put asunder."[19]

The biblical account of the origin of things has for its primary purpose to tell us about God's plan. It is not meant to give us a course in prehistory and paleontology. That is why we must interpret the words of Genesis, and also Christ's reference to it, as being concerned with the nature of marriage. It remains possible that monogamous marriage is the fruit of a development, but then such a development is the expression of a law of nature and an order of creation; hence it may not be undone.

---

[17]Gen. 2, 24.
[18]Mark 10, 4-7.
[19]Matt. 19, 4-7.

On the other hand, the history of marriage does not show solely a progressive ascent. At times, there is a retrogression or an arrest. The Mosaic Law tolerated those things, as Christ said, "by reason of the hardness of your heart."[20] If there is an evolution of marriage, this evolution is also influenced by sin that entered our world. However, when Christ restores God's plan, this implies that He also restores the relation to salvation in which the human heart is opened up for the personal love demanded by monogamous and indissoluble marriage. Marriage, then, attains in Him the fullness of its relation to God.

MARRIAGE AND COVENANT

Mankind has projected many images of the communion which God offers to it, but man's ancient temptation to try to become like to God by his own efforts has greatly influenced his ideas about that communion. We find all sort of myths about marriages between gods and men and about their offspring. All this had to disappear when clearness came through Israel in man's dialogue with God. Yahweh is known first as the inaccessible God of Sinai, who allies Himself with His people in virtue of His sovereign election. This He does, not by a fusion of nature, but by a personal and historical encounter. Only after this has been made clear, does Yahweh show Himself also in His kindness, as a Father for His firstborn. His people can now look upon Him also as on a Bridegroom, or rather as a Husband. Only once, and in a passing way, are the imperfect, polygamous traits of the human marriage of the time applied to Yahweh's relations with His people.[21] But from Osee to the Canticle of Canticles, the sacred writers express chiefly the personal wedded love of God for His only spouse. Osee especially gives us the touching description of Yahweh's fidelity in spite of the "adultery" of His people. In the Canticle, we read how God's fidelity finally overcame the infidelity of His spouse.

---

[20]Mark 10, 5; Matt. 19, 8.
[21]Exech. 23, 4. "And I took them and they bore sons and daughters."

112

In the New Testament, the role of the bridegroom or husband is totally transferred to Christ. Now His bride or wife is the new Israel, the Church, as a local community,[22] or more often in its entirety.[23] This relation of the glorified Christ to His Church is important for the proper appreciation of marriage within the Church, even more so than what Christ said about marriage during His life on earth.

Christian marriage in fact is doubly related to Christ's union with the Church: it is a reflection of this union and is also taken up into it. In the Old Testament, human marriage was the starting point for speaking about the Covenant between Yahweh and Israel, but in St. Paul the relation is in reverse. Here the union between the Incarnate Word and the Church, the Covenant, which can so much more legitimately be called a marriage on account of the Incarnation, is itself the prototype that shows what marriage between Christians actually is or rather what it should be. It is an example of loving surrender and reception. Hence it is also a model for the most profound union that is possible on the human level (cf. Eph. 5).

But marriage between Christians not only looks up to the example given by the union of Christ and His Church. It is also taken up into that Covenant and, in a sense, traversed by it. The relation of the Church to her Lord and Bridegroom is proper to every Christian, for the Church does not float above us, as it were, but exists in us.

Today, we are inclined to attribute the nuptial relation with Christ at most to the soul, but St. Paul[24] here names precisely the body: "The body is . . . for the Lord and the Lord for the body." The last part of the sentence which expresses the reciprocity of the relationship, shows that we all belong to Christ in a nuptial manner, for we have here in the body the same reciprocity of belonging which was announced by St.

---

[22]"For I am jealous for you with a divine jealousy. For I betrothed you to one spouse." 2 Cor. 11, 2.
[23]Eph. 5, 25-32; Apoc. 21, 2, 9.
[24]1 Cor. 6, 13.

Paul with respect to husband and wife.[25] Hence the relation between two married Christians is taken up into the Covenant of Christ and His Church and also is "traversed" by it.

All this is very meaningful for Christian marriage, and there is much that the Church has gradually appreciated more and more in the course of the centuries and to which she has given expression. It is a basis for the sacramental character of marriage, of which we shall speak later.

We must now draw attention to two aspects which are immediately connected with what we have just described. The first is the superiority of the marriage that is entirely "in Christ" over the marriage that is merely a preparation for it. It is true, the marriage of the unbaptized must not be looked upon as being purely "natural," any more than the other elements of their life, for there are no voids in the history of salvation of mankind. There are, however, areas of development. There is an ascent to the full community with Christ and His Church. This is so because all that is human attains its full unfolding in Christ and His Church, and remains open to this unfolding as long as it has not yet attained that goal.

Keeping this in mind, we can understand why St. Paul does not consider the married person who is converted to the faith to be bound to his or her marriage if the unbelieving partner wants to depart.[26] This we usually call the "Pauline privilege." We must note that the Apostle has stated earlier that, if the unbeliever consents to live with the Christian partner, the believer must also consent. Separation can be granted for the sake of fidelity to the faith. It is not meant to become a sanction for human infidelity.

Christian marriage has won a very high place as a state of life. But there is another Christian state of life in which Christ's union with the Church is not merely imitated but is directly lived. In this state, there is a renunciation of mar-

---

[25] "The wife has not authority over her body, but the husband; the husband likewise has not authority over his body, but the wife." 1 Cor. 7, 4.

[26] "If the unbeliever departs, let him depart." 1 Cor. 7, 15.

riage.   Here virginity is chosen for Christ's sake and the nuptial bond between Christ and the Church is expressed by foregoing something, by living that bond itself immediately. St. Paul says that the choice of the state of virginity is "better" than that of marriage,[27] and the Council of Trent took over and repeated that teaching.[28]

The Apostle adds, however, that each one has his own "gift" in that respect.[29]   The sublimity of the more direct bond with Christ does not detract in any way from the sacredness that must be attributed to marriage because of its particular status, as we have just explained.   That is why a Council of Asia Minor condemned those who chose virginity out of contempt for marriage.   Neither, on the other hand, should the state of virginity be chosen purely on account of its higher value in the abstract, for each person should try to find out what is reserved for him or her.   A life of virginity is not of itself more meritorious, for merit does not depend on the state in which we are, but on the love that animates our life.   After saying this, we may demand that married people also will have enough respect for the state of virginity to encourage their children, if they are called to that state.   Christian parents will test such a vocation, but should not exclude it *a priori.*

THE SACRAMENT OF MARRIAGE

The books of the New Testament, as we have seen, say profound things about the *state* of marriage.   They do not say one word about marriage being a sacrament.   Not only is the term "sacrament" not used,[30] but—unlike the case of Baptism and the Eucharist—they do not mention any rite which

---

[27]1 Cor. 7, 38.

[28]Denzinger, No. 980.

[29]"I would that you all were as I am myself; but each one has his own gift from God, one in this way, and another in that." 1 Cor. 7, 7.

[30]In Ephesians 5, 32 marriage is called *mysterion,* in Latin *sacramentum,* but the term does not have the meaning of what we today call a "sacrament."

we can recognize as a sacrament. Nevertheless, the Council of Trent is of the opinion that Chapter Five of St. Paul's Epistle to the Ephesians suggests[31] the sacramental nature of marriage. We should like to say the same thing about the ideas St. Paul expressed in the sixth and seventh chapter of First Corinthians.

We are accustomed to base ourselves on a definition of a sacrament as being an outward sign which both signifies and gives grace in virtue of being instituted by Christ. However, we ask ourselves whether every word of man to man and every interpersonal symbolic act of man does not signify and impart human communion. Likewise, we ask whether every message and every sign of consecration or of a union in the Church, which is Christ's Body, does not therefore signify and impart the divine-human communion or life of grace. If this is true, something should be added to the definition of the sacrament, in order to distinguish the seven "sacraments" from the other signs of grace existing in the Church. We would then define those sacraments as signs that give grace, in which Christ's bestowal of salvation on His Church is depicted in the interplay of minister and recipient, and in which there is at the same time a relation to the pivotal moments of our life.

When the sacraments are conceived in this way, the texts of the New Testament about the marriage state strongly suggest that the marriage contract is a sacrament. If, according to Chapter Five of Ephesians, man and woman reciprocally represent Christ and the Church in their entire married life, they certainly represent them also in the symbolic act with which they begin that life. In other words, they are reciprocally ministers and recipients of a sacrament.

On the other hand, when a person chooses the state of virginity, this too is a union, but Christ now does *not* appear in another *human being*. The virgin binds herself directly to Christ and at the same time renounces any other partner. On that account, this union is not a sacrament as defined

---

[31]*"innuit."* See Denzinger, No. 969.

116

above, however holy it might otherwise be for the one who is called to that state.

There is, moreover, the considerable role which the nuptial bond plays in human life. The more a Christian is personally involved in an activity, the more his Lord is involved in it and the more that activity takes place in Him. Now the surrender of one human being to another "in the body," that is, in the entire incarnate personality, is incomparably more central and intimate than any other union. It is precisely in this sphere that the Christian is spoken to by his Lord, that he is taken up in a marriage with Him: "The body is for the Lord and the Lord for the body."[32]

From this, St. Paul concludes that adultery is unlawful, but it follows also that for a Christian there is no true or lawful marriage when the Lord is not involved in it, when it is not, as St. Paul explains further on, a marrying "in the Lord."[33] This marrying in the Lord can then be conceived precisely as an alliance undertaken explicitly on the basis of Christ, as a sacrament.

These considerations can serve to explain the decisive fact that the Church accepts the marriage contract as a rite that is comparable to baptism, confirmation, etc., in short, as one of the seven sacraments. It is only in the early Middle Ages that those seven signs were thus singled out on account of their special place and role and that the term "sacrament" was reserved for them. This recognition is fully expressed in the definitions formulated by the Council of Trent, which declares that there are seven sacraments and that marriage is a sacrament.[34]

It is easier for us to understand the gradual manifestation of this last sacrament when we ask ourselves, starting from the point we have now reached in history: What precisely could we expect as the sacramental sign of marriage? The answer is, "nothing in particular." Christian marriage can

[32]1 Cor. 5, 14.
[33]1 Cor. 7, 39.
[34]Denzinger, nos. 844, 971.

adopt any sign which in a particular culture is considered to be the expression of the intention of man and woman to bind themselves as husband and wife, provided their action in some way has a relation to their being Christians.

This hypothesis is based on the forms which the marriage contract still can have today, even in the Latin Church. Of course, there is the rigorous prescription of the Council of Trent regarding the presence of the pastor and two witnesses; otherwise the contract is invalid. But there are also other possibilities in case this precept cannot be observed. There can be a valid marriage that is not contracted before a priest, when it is impossible to obtain his presence within one month.[35] There is even a forging of the bond that is merely implicit in the continued living-together, either when a *sanatio in radice* is granted, or when two married persons both receive baptism. In the latter case, we can say that the sacramental union is contained in the combination of their baptism and the continuation of their life together. If, therefore, the sacrament of marriage can be implicit in such a way, it seems that the form it has, in virtue of its institution, is not more definite than what we have just indicated.

The case of married persons who both receive baptism is less frequent today in Christian countries, but it must have been very frequent in early times, when child baptism was still relatively rare. This explains, to a certain extent, why the books of the New Testament do not contain anything regarding a rite of Christian marriage. There is also the fact that a very long time elapsed, even after the apostolic times, before such a rite arose.

At first, the wedding among Christians took place, as among pagans, in the family, and Christians surrounded their own weddings with prayers. Because the priest had control over the validity of a marriage, before he would allow a husband and a wife to be present at Mass, there arose the custom of having the marriage contracted before the priest and other witnesses, first in front of, and later within, the

---

[35]Code of Canon Law, Canon 1098.

church building. The Council of Trent, in order to prevent clandestine marriages, made the wedding before the pastor and two witnesses obligatory, and in normal cases its validity depends on those conditions. Added to these are various rites, some of which are of Roman and Germanic origin, such as the giving of rings. Following the custom introduced in Germany, various countries have adopted an appropriate ceremony in the vernacular.

The exchange of blessed rings between bride and groom, which is prescribed in some new rituals, expresses very well the reciprocal nature of the marriage contract and the ritual emphasizes that man and woman are the ministers of the sacrament, whereas the priest functions as one of the witnesses. Moreover, the priest, along with the official witnesses, involves also the whole community of the faithful in what is taking place. Finally, the whole ceremony does not precede the celebration of Mass, but is taken up into it. In particular, a special blessing is given to the spouses after the *Pater Noster,* and the Mass is followed by a special exhortation.

We have tried to show the importance of the nuptial bond between Christ and His Church for the marriage between two Christians, in order to get a better understanding of the sacramentality of Christian marriage. There is another point which will perhaps be better understood by starting from this same bond. We mean the specifically Christian element contained in chastity. This we can express first and best by saying a word about "immorality" or fornication.

The Old Testament forbade misconduct or adultery in the sixth of the Ten Commandments. As we mentioned already, sex relations between members of one family were also forbidden as fornication or "immorality," which practically meant incest. There was question here of human relations, those of an existing marriage or blood relationship, which had to be respected by refraining from sexual intercourse.

Because of a more refined reverence for the human relations involved in sexual intercourse, we realize today that no one should engage in sexual relationship without a bond that guarantees the complete personal commitment of the partners and their responsibility for the child. In other words, there should be no such relationship except within a marriage. Moreover, the sexual union attains its moral goodness only if the partner meets the other as a person and gives respect and love accordingly. To treat the other as an "object," as a "thing," is, to the extent it is done, unchaste, even when it takes place within a lawful marriage. We appreciate all this in the measure in which we have a more refined feeling for the fact that the other is a fellow human being. These are the human aspects of chastity.

St. Paul, moreover, reveals the specific Christian aspect of chastity when he says, as we have already recalled: "The body is for the Lord and the Lord for the body."[36] Respect for Christ in the other, in virtue of which the most profound incarnate surrender, the one that takes place in the sexual sphere, can take place only in the Lord, is chastity in its Christian practice. That is why it can be called the "holy virtue," but not at all in the oppressive sense that was so frequently attached to that term in former days.

Christian chastity is neither the all-embracing nor the principal virtue. This title belongs to love. Chastity is love insofar as it sees in man precisely the consecration to Christ. This demand of chastity stands out clearly in betrothal. When man and woman have finally reached the point where they promise fidelity for life and become engaged, what is there that still stands in the way of translating that promise into sexual union? It is not that by intercourse they degrade the person of the beloved and make him or her an "object." But sexual union is still out of place, because there is not yet an objective and socially binding obligation which safeguards all the consequences of sex relationship. For the Christian, however, the principal reason is that the alliance is not yet fully in the Lord, that Christ Himself has not yet given these two to each other. This does not mean that

---

[36]1 Cor. 6, 13.

betrothal is purely negative. It rather reveals precisely its deepest significance as the common preparation of both partners for the sacrament, a preparation which consists also in their growth toward each other as authentic human beings.

MARRIAGE AS SOCIETY AND AS COMMUNITY

The Old Testament, perfected in Christ's preaching, gave clearness to monogamy. The relation between the risen Lord and His Church constitutes the background for St. Paul's statements and suggestions concerning the state of Christian marriage. From these scriptural data, the post-apostolic tradition slowly developed its view regarding the sacramentality of the marriage contract and gave stature to this sacrament.

We have described the phases of the history of salvation regarding marriage in view of our modern interest in it. The history of salvation has not come to a standstill. In a certain sense, the supernatural truths concerning marriage have already been duly expressed, though they are still matter for ever more profound thought and study. Supernatural truths, however, are not concerned with a separate sector of reality. On the contrary, they provide an interpretation of our entire human existence in our whole world. Such an interpretation, from the standpoint of our relation to God in Christ, needs to be given in a new form and in a more profound way at this time when our human existence and our world undergo so great a process of change. Today we are acquiring an unforeseen technological control over nature and also over our own bodily existence, and we are especially aware of the personal character of man. On that account, our Faith is asked now to explain the meaning and purpose of marriage in a more profound way.

Man is a being in whom nature pursues its own ends, but he is also a person. He is both at the same time; he is a person *in* his work and his struggle for existence. From the dark beginnings of mankind, there have been preserved not only skeletons but also tools, the first hesitant announcement of man's dominion over nature. Much later times reveal man's wonder and emotion, in which he stands revealed as a person. He now lives his own life and exercises his own activity as one who is not subordinate to another end. Man is consciously a person, and therefore an end in himself, in what today we call "disinterested" activity. The Greeks were the first to discern this and to strive for it separately, assigning "contemplation" to free man and labor to slaves. This "contemplation" developed into culture.

In the time of liberalism, which is at least partly behind us, culture was for the happy few and work was for the masses. Today we are coming nearer to equalization. On the one hand, even the "liberal professions" are taken up in the process of work, in the common building of our world. On the other hand, room and time are in the process of being provided for all, to enable them to pursue "disinterested" undertakings and to be together with others for "disinterested" non-utilitarian ends.

This shows, at the same time, that both levels in the actualization of our human existence are connected with our fellow-men. In the work of producing and acquiring goods, men join in some form of "society" which is always defined by the specific purpose to be reached. The common contemplative and cultural expression, on the other hand, leads to a "community." A community is an end in itself. It consists in knowing one another and in accepting one another as an end in itself.

It is unavoidable that those two forms of human existence should also find expression in marriage. The high point of Greek culture is at the same time the low point with respect to married life. The husband thought of his wife as merely someone who gave him children and kept his house. For sexual relations on the personal level, he preferred the company of "hetaerae" and boys.

We meet a much more human married life in the world described by Homer and also in that of the Bible. Jacob dearly loves Rachel and Samuel similarly loves Anna, although that which is expressly praised in a good woman has a somewhat utilitarian ring. It is sufficient to recall in this context the song of praise of the valiant woman in the Book of Proverbs (ch. 31). She is more an aid than a companion.

It is our time once more that places in sharpest contrast to each other, within marriage and the family, the concept of the utilitarian society and that of a disinterested community. The family is no longer a society of labor. It has lost its social function, and in the coming technological world it will either be dissolved or appear as a community of persons.

In western society, the patriarchal family is on the decline, in the sense that young couples no longer establish themselves in the family of their parents. They have their own separate dwelling. There is also an almost complete independence in the choice of a mate. This reminds us of the fact that not only the sacramental sign by which the will to marry or "consent" is expressed in various cultures can vary, but also that there may be diversity even in that consent itself. Formerly, there were marriages in which a young person, especially the girl, abided by the choice made by the parents—which choice they personally accepted —and such marriages were perfectly valid in that cultural system. Today we require a personal choice which, in principle, means independence from others.

The Church, in our present world situation, faces some cultures, as for instance in Africa, in which life is regulated —though perhaps not much longer so—by the clan, and it is the clan that determines the choice of a mate. In such a situation, it is not proper to try to impose our modern western standard of freedom. On the other hand, there is our modern western way regarding the choice of a mate— a way which perhaps will soon be universally adopted. The Church must accept this pattern, but at the same time protect the choice against specifically modern types of immaturity.

There are evidences of such immaturity. We see this, for instance, when young people have already begotten a child and then enter the marriage state, under social pressure, solely in order "to save the situation." Here we notice another danger that is the reverse side of a great good. In virtue of the change described above, marriage is entered upon more and more, and life is lived in it, as in a community of love, hence as an end in itself. Philosophers like Gustave Thibon have warned us against the one-sidedness that can enter here. There is nothing wrong with a "marriage of love" that is also a "marriage of reason." In fact, the latter serves precisely as a protection for a community of love. The love of married people includes sexual attraction, but it is not reduced to that. That is why genuine married love does not cease when feeling disappears. On the contrary, it grows stronger through unselfish fidelity.

In our own day, love is often reduced to sexual attraction. This has created a situation in which the question whether it is lawful to separate from one's partner "for any reason at all" is asked as insistently as in Christ's day, and many refuse to believe in Christ's answer. It is not divorce that can safeguard marriage as a community of love, but fidelity that matures in a "night of the senses." The latter has been wonderfully expressed by J. H. Walgrave:

> There are people who fit well together, but when they meet with a crisis in their sexual attraction or feeling, they move apart and suffer the deepest sort of human frustration for the rest of their lives. We realize what that leads to. In almost all married lives there is, sooner or later, a crisis in the sexual attraction and feeling of the partners. All emotional life has its periods of aridity. Such crises have a normal significance for the growth of human personality. They contain an invitation to the partners to purify, deepen and strengthen their attitude toward each other.
>
> This temporary divergence of the attitude of will and the sphere of sensuous feelings acts as an invitation to the partners to enter into the depths of their own personality and to reshape their whole attitude to each other on

a higher level. It is understandable that romantic love, which is unstable, carries off two people who enter marriage in a blissful experience that engages their personalities.

The crisis of sexuality and sensibility is a period of transition in which personal love, which requires constancy, must be firmly established and take the lead in order to inspire the language of feeling and the sensuous mutual attraction in a new way. Just as the rocket first carries off the missile which then follows its own independent path, so does the erotic attraction first carry off personal love according to its own direction, in order that later this love may lead its own life in the settled ways of a personal community. Married love, like divine love, has its mystical night and this night is the transition to a brighter day.

Fickle romantic love must give way to the more peaceful and extensive family love in which personal attachment, ever new and fresh, resounds in a peaceful emotion of the heart and the senses. The development of the relations between husband and wife is therefore a progressive growing into a true communion of persons and a less ecstatic but more profound happiness.[37]

The Meaning of Marriage

It goes without saying that, when married life is lived as a disinterested communion of love, there is then a problem regarding its being directed toward the multiplication of the race. Church Law and Church Authority declare that the latter is the primary end of marriage; other ends are secondary. Does that mean that the personal communion of love is thereby reduced to the rank of a means?

It is our opinion that such Church pronouncements do not take away the value of the married union as an act of personal communion, for the simple reason that they do not consider it as such. Perhaps we are permitted to say—and we shall express this more precisely further on—that the

[37]J. H. Walgrave "Dialectiek van het huwelijk." *Kultuurleven,* vol. 25 (1958), pp. 165-176. The quotation is from page 173. See also Adrian L. van Kaam, "The Fantasy of Romantic Love," *Modern Myths and Popular Fancies,* Pittsburgh, 1961, pp. 24-48.

official pronouncements of the Church view marriage solely as a society and institution. Hence they express the hierarchy of ends in this society, making procreation take precedence over the others.

We said already that woman in the Old Testament was considered principally as an aid to man. This does not mean that human procreation was left out of consideration. In the second chapter of Genesis, marriage is considered solely within the perspective of the unity between man and woman, whereas being-man-and-woman, as considered in the account of Creation in Chapter One of Genesis, is connected with the command "Increase and multiply" as is done also after the Flood, in the ninth chapter of Genesis.[38] Children are "the inheritance of the Lord."[39] Childlessness, on the contrary, is seen as a frustration and a punishment in most books of the Old Testament.[40] It stands to reason that the married partners in normal circumstances have also the task of cooperating in procuring a progeny of children. This finds expression only on the occasion of the measures that are taken in particular situations to insure a progeny. For instance, there was the union of a man with the slave-woman of his wife, and the obligatory marriage between a brother-in-law and a childless widow.

In the texts of the New Testament which we have quoted, there is likewise question only about the community of husband and wife, although, on the other hand, St. Paul also explicitly describes the task of the wife as that of childbearing.[41] The Bible does not attach any philosophy about ends and means to the mutual help of, and procreation by, the partners. This was done only by medieval scholastics, who made the aspect of mutual help appear as subordinate to that of procreation.

This is also the fundamental position in the later pronouncements by the Church. These are summed up in one sentence

---

[38]Gen. 1, 28; Gen. 9, 7.
[39]Ps. 126, 3.
[40]Gen. 30; 1 Sam. 1, 6-18; Is. 47-9; Jer. 18, 21.
[41]1 Tim. 2, 15; 5, 14.

of the Church's Code of Canon Law: "The primary purpose of marriage is the procreation and education of children; the secondary purpose is the mutual help and protection against the abuse of sex life."[42] Many declarations of Pius XI and Pius XII stress and defend this doctrine. It is also upheld in the famous Encyclical *Casti Connubii (Christian Marriage)*, which merely adds a consideration on another level without any reflection on the interconnection.

Before speaking about this other consideration, we should like to underscore the truth contained in those declarations *on their own level*, which is that of the purposive action in a society and not that of the disinterested togetherness in a community of persons. Man is taken up in the cosmos, in nature, in the progress and ascent of life on earth which fulfills itself in him. This idea is most powerfully expressed today in the work of Teilhard de Chardin. Now, in this progress of life, the new being is that to which the parents tend. In higher forms of life, living nature strives for its perpetuation in new individuals through the union of male and female. This is true also of human beings. However, we have here a "hominized" way—namely, the communion of man and woman in a human act that tends to produce as its fruit a new human being. That is why rearing children, and specifically a long process of human education, belongs to that task.

On the Christian level, this purposiveness means that the sexual communion, actualized precisely in the sphere of genital sexuality, is directed to the child and that this orientation should be consciously acknowledged and respected. Man must accept his biological nature in a human way and therefore involve himself in the whole finality of life.

We should now go on to consider the plane of the personal community as such, but we must first give more precision to what we have stated above. Two remarks are in order. First, man is a free being and as such he is allowed to aim in the first instance at the subordinate or secondary end. That which determines the direction to be taken is

---

[42]Canon 1913, par. 1.

often that which man aims at last in his action. As the classical saying goes: "that which is first in intention is the last in execution."

Married people may, in all peace of conscience, aim first at their mutual fulfillment. They then assent to the purpose of procreation by their openness toward it, or, to express it in a more manageable formula, by not excluding procreation. Hence the Church's teaching that procreation is the primary purpose of marriage is also most intimately connected with another doctrine—and we say *doctrine* and not "positive command"—namely, that it is unlawful to use contraceptives.

Our second remark is to the effect that marriage relations between husband and wife do not on that account become a *mere* means, even on the plane of purpose. The Church in her documents speaks of a secondary *end,* and she declares that artificial insemination is as unlawful as contraceptive practices. This shows that sexual intercourse has not merely and exclusively the value of a means, so that it can be replaced by any other way of procuring procreation. Marriage relations are irreplaceable because, besides their value as means, they have a value of their own.

Even when we abstract from the consideration of personal communion, it seems to us that the sex relationship has its own proper value, for nothing exists that is a pure means. We believe that a "pure" means is an abstraction, and rather a mathematical than a metaphysical abstraction. It is something comparable to the "straight line," which likewise never exists in reality.

We ask ourselves whether there is anything that is purely a means even among "things." At least, man makes things not merely to serve as tools but also beautiful in themselves. Still less do we find in the order of living beings things that are purely directed to a purpose. Here we find rather a wealth of flowers and a superabundance of seeds. Bisexuality likewise is not solely for the purpose of procreation. In lower beings, reproduction is accomplished also by mere fission. Where the bisexual process takes place, it certainly proves to be better adapted for procreation, but this is not its only meaning. By mating, the individuals themselves are quickened and enlivened. All this is present also, on a higher level, in man. Sexual life not only makes generation possible, but it also gives man and woman a biological and psychological development, which thereby integrates the sexual urge and protects it against possible deviation. It is thus a "protection against the abuse of sex life" which, for that matter, fully functions only when it is integrated on the plane of love. "The mutual assistance" of the partners in marriage is also a mutual vitalization. That is why it is rightly said to be something more than a means and is called a secondary *end.*

It is time, however, that we go over to the higher plane of the person and his or her disinterested community life, the plane of love. This aspect also has always been present in Scripture and Tradition, either in the background or more in the foreground. We pointed out already that in the Old Testament there appears to be not only cooperation of the partners, but love also. Otherwise, those who lived at that time could not even have seen in human marriage an image of Yahweh's faithful and tender love for Israel. When Jesus proclaims the indissolubility of marriage, in addition to monogamy, He makes marriage be precisely a community of persons. When St. Paul, in the fifth chapter of Ephesians, presents Christ's relation to the Church as the model for married people, he thereby describes the love that has its own reason and resting-point in that community of persons.

That is why Tradition considers in marriage not only the division of labor among the partners, but also the community of love. For example, St. Augustine formulates the classical description of the "blessings of marriage," saying that they are: "offspring, conjugal faith and the sacrament." In the official pronouncements of the Church, we find the clearest expression of marriage as being a community of love, in the well-known words of the Encyclical *Casti Connubii* of Pius XI:

This mutual interior formation of the partners, this earnest desire of perfecting one another, can be said in a certain very true sense, as the *Roman Catechism* teaches, to be the primary cause and reason of marriage (*primaria matrimonii causa et ratio*)—if only marriage is taken not strictly as an institution for the proper procreation and education of children, but in a broader sense as a sharing, a community, a union of their whole life (*totius vitae communio, consuetudo, societas*).[43]

Especially the last words—in which "societas" is evidently *not* conceived in contrast to "communitas" or "communio"— show us that marriage is not thought of here as a society that is formed for a definite purpose, but as a community of persons that has its meaning in itself. It has, as such, an end or meaning that is called primary and is evidently not subordinate to procreation.

Is this contrary to the thesis that procreation is the primary purpose of marriage, as is also proclaimed a few lines before in *Casti connubii*? It is not. The proposition that procreation is the primary end of marriage refers to marriage taken strictly and specifically as marriage. The new position of *Casti connubii* touches marriage inasmuch as it is considered only in a wider sense as a community of life, and not in a specific but a generic sense, hence insofar as it resembles friendship, for example.

By saying this, it seems that we have posed a problem rather than solving one. For, if the human person constitutes a unity, if it does not exist alongside but *in* the body, and if the personal love of husband and wife becomes incarnate *in* their sexual intercourse, we are then faced with the question of how that community of persons is embodied in married life. Does marriage, as a personal community in love, also have anything to do with procreation, or is the latter a mere purpose (*Zweck*) on the practical level? Hence does procreation lie on a lower level than the meaning (*Sinn*) of the com-

---

[43]"Casti Connubii," *Acta Apostolicae Sedis,* vol. XXII (1930), p. 548.

munity of love, as was maintained in the famous thesis of Doms?[44]

The Church's teaching authority has explicitly rejected that conclusion, but a positive answer to the question we have enunciated is still to be formulated. The following ideas are offered here as a step toward such a reply.

Man is one: his bodily being in the world, his being involved in nature and in life, is personal existence. Conversely, he is an embodied person, and realizes himself as person in his nature. We can therefore expect that *both* purposes mentioned above in connection with the lower level of marriage, are also found on the level of the personal community.

When we no longer consider the community of love of husband and wife in a broad and general sense, as is done in *Casti Connubii,* but pay attention to its specific realization in marriage, the orientation to procreation will inevitably play its role. The communion of love becomes incarnate in sexuality and specifically in the deepest intimacy of genital sexuality. Hence that community of love must also have a genital aspect.

Someone could perhaps object that we once more make the person and the personal community subordinate to a practical end. Our viewpoint, one might fear, puts into jeopardy the personalistic character of marriage. Having been granted a hesitant recognition in *Casti connubii,* it will now get lost among the other pronouncements of the Church which so rarely emphasize the personal aspect of marriage. We shall try to answer that objection by making the following three remarks.

First, the "disinterested" activities in which we display our personal existence are not subordinate to any other end, yet they are not on that account useless in other fields of our life. To use, or rather enjoy leisure, to be together

---

[44]Herbert Doms, *The Meaning of Marriage,* New York, 1939. Cf. John C. Ford, "Marriage: Its Meaning and Purposes," *Theological Studies* Vol. III (September 1942) pp. 333-374.

at home or with friends, to play, to enjoy beautiful things, are not directly for the purpose of enabling us to do better work. In fact, we spoil those things when we subordinate them to that purpose. Nevertheless, those activities are fruitful precisely because they are disinterested, for they raise our whole human existence, and hence also our work, to a higher level.

The same must be said about the connection between human relations and labor, between pure science and material progress, between culture and technology, between prayer and our professional duties.

This leads us to the *second* point—that the fruit of such "disinterested" activities is given with those things themselves. This fruit is not pursued as an ulterior end, but it is gratefully accepted in the activity which experiences and expresses our personal being. It is co-intended with that activity and included therein. For the application of this idea to marriage, we may quote again J. P. Walgrave:

> The enriching of the personal community, to the extent that the earthly situation of husband and wife offers an opportunity for it, is essentially co-intended in the love which they have for each other. That enrichment is an expression of their love. *Within the personal community of marriage, the orientation of both partners to the child is not another orientation than that of husband and wife to each other.* Both desire the full personal good of the other. This personal good is the human perfection in disinterested service and loving responsibility. They make one another respectively a father and a mother and thus give each other the noblest task of love and care, by which they can mature and grow as persons. The purpose of nature is thus incorporated in the purpose of the community of persons, and the dialectical antithesis is resolved in a complete synthesis by which the mutual love of husband and wife and their creative love for the child are fused into one love.[45]

---

[45]"Dialectiek van het huwelijk," *Kultuurleven,* Vol. 25, (1958), pp. 174 ff. (Italics are ours.)

We come now to the *third* point. The fruit of the matrimonial community of persons is not a material product, it is the child. The child is not merely given existence, but is called to be a person. Hence the child is the extension of the personal community of the parents to their children.

Let us add a few words regarding this last aspect. There is only one perfect community of persons, that of the Father, the Son, and the Holy Ghost. This divine community too has openness, but in virtue of its pure riches and a free bestowal of love: It wishes to take us also into Its life. Every other community of persons has openness, both because it tends to diffuse its riches and because it is itself in need of completion. This is true even of the community of the Blessed before the Last Judgment at the Coming of Christ. For they "were told to rest a little while longer, until the number of their fellow-servants and their brethren . . . should be complete."[46]

This idea holds true even more with respect to mankind upon earth and the Church. Mankind spreads in ever new generations, because it gives of its riches but also because it must grow to greater fullness of being-human. The same can be said of the Church, for new members, and particularly new peoples, that come to her, will not only attain their salvation through her, but will also contribute "to the mature measure of the fullness of Christ."[47]

The same idea applies in its own way to the smaller human communities of love. Love ceases to be love when it is merely an *"égoisme à deux,"* a selfish association of two. All true friendship makes the friends to be full of love in their contacts with others. The same holds true with respect to the bond of love between husband and wife, but here the most characteristic way in which their communion with others is expressed is the "formation" of a family. We use the last term on purpose, because "procreation," "generation" and certainly "reproduction" point too exclusively to the biological plane.

---

[46]Apoc. 6, 11.
[47]Eph. 4, 13.

In the family, the community of husband and wife grows and develops into the community of parents and children not only because children are begotten, born and bred, but also because the person which each child is becomes a sharer in the parental community of love. In married persons, the human race builds itself, not only as a biological species, but principally as a community of persons. In Christian marriage also, the Church builds herself up as a community of love, although other sacraments, and first of all baptism, must be added to it. The unity of mutual love and that fruitfulness on the personal plane are such that the married partners, by their "giving" love to their children, at the same time complete each other to the full humanness of parenthood. We see then that marriage, as a disinterested community of persons, has a single meaning that can be described as the love that makes husband and wife become parents and as the fruitfulness that enlarges the community of those who love.

CHAPTER FIVE

LABOR AND THE WORLD OF LABOR

Our present world is an industrial world. North America, Western Europe, and the Soviet Union are already largely industrialized, and other peoples are busy learning from western industrialization in order to emancipate themselves from western colonialism. Through industrialization, labor has acquired a new form and has, moreover, attained to a new place in human existence. The workers constitute a new class, or perhaps more accurately, a new rank and certainly a new type of man. In addition, there is in the whole of society an ever growing rational division of labor and in the same measure everybody becomes a worker. Work is looked upon more and more as the duty of everyone and it puts its stamp on the life of all.

All this demands a confrontation of work with the Church. Since the beginning of our century and until recently, that encounter was confined to a clarification of the economic and social position of the laborer. Even now, there are still many areas, even in the western world, in which such a clarification is necessary. At the same time, something more profound is asked of the Church. It is not only necessary to clarify the struggle for better living conditions, but the whole ethos of labor must be confronted with our faith. The Church must once more encounter the mass of the workers who, especially in Europe and South America, have abandoned her because they have been neglected and misunderstood, not only in their social struggle, but even in their human existence as laborers. Not only the organization of laborers, but their very work, must find a place in the plan of salvation. This means also that their community must meet Christ and the Church, not merely on the organization level, but much more deeply, as the whole working community of men, as the whole world of industry.

135

In some countries, for example in Holland, the form of pastoral care devoted to this encounter is known as "industrial apostolate" and its Protestant counterpart is appropriately called "Gospel and Industry." The care of souls on that level demands a special message and approach. Hence we need a theology of work and of the world of labor. Attempts have been made to arrive at such a theology, although it still consists mostly of introductory programs or tentative essays.[1]

The formation of such a theology is not an easy task. The theme of human labor crops up only incidentally in Scripture and Tradition. No commandment of the Decalogue prescribes labor. Hence catechisms that divide moral teaching according to the Ten Commandments don't know what place should be given to the duty of work. No doubt, there are enough exhortations to work in Scripture. Both the texts of the Old Testament and the example of St. Paul and especially of Christ Himself in the New Testament have contributed to a Christian esteem for work which differs from the concepts prevalent in the Greco-Roman world.

Nevertheless, we ask ourselves whether labor itself, and not merely the workman, has been sufficiently appreciated in Christian thinking. Have we overcome the Greek lack of esteem for work and are we able to meet the Marxist with his excessive esteem for it?

The Bible begins with the description of the children and grandchildren of Adam as cattle-breeders, farmers, town dwellers, and manual workers, but we aren't given the impression that man developed slowly through his labor into the man of culture he has now been for many thousands of

---

[1]For example M. D. Chenu, *Pour une théologie du travail*, Paris, 1953; H. Rondet, *Die Theologie der Arbeit*, Würzburg, 1955; M. D. Chenu, A. de Bovis, H. Rondet, *L'enfant et son avenir professionnel. Perspectives théologiques*, Paris, 1959. Important also are more general works, such as, G. Thils, *Théologie des réalités terrestres*, 2 vols. Paris, 1949. Regarding the spirituality of work, cf. R. Guelluy; *Le travail dans la vie du chrétien*, Brussels, 1953; P. Teilhard de Chardin. *The Divine Milieu*, New York, 1969; E. Rideau, *Consécration*, Paris, 1946; E. Rideau "Teaching the Christian Attitude to Work and Suffering," *Lumen Vitae*, vol. 9 (1954), pp. 303-314.

years. The Bible does not disclose to what extent labor has been a factor in making us men.

It is only by studying history and by philosophical reflection that we are able to discern the exact place and role of work in our existence and then construct a Christian ethos of labor that goes beyond incidental admonitions. Hence a theology of labor cannot be satisfied with the few data contained in the sources of Revelation. It must be based also on an anthropological study of labor.

We act perfectly in accord with Revelation itself when we use our mental powers to judge and analyze things, for Revelation, especially in the New Testament, is not intended to give us a collection of rules of conduct, but a light of the Spirit. With these helps, we should try to figure out, on the basis of nature and our situation, in what way we must translate into concrete life our participation in Christ's obedience to the Father. That is why we wish to begin with some anthropological considerations of labor and thus gradually get a better idea of the role it plays in the plan of salvation.

What is Labor?

When we survey historical times, we find that in the ancient cultures of the East heavy work was done by slaves and by farmers, herdsmen, and manual workers, and these were judged to belong to the lower classes. The Greeks added the idea that contemplation is the ideal of a free man. In the early Middle Ages, work, which was still largely agricultural, was not only better appreciated throughout society, but also gave a new shape to the home-life and the whole existence of those workers. The trade or craft ennobled man. That situation lasted until the appearance of the steam engine.

When man transferred part of his work to an independent machine, he thereby became its complement and servant. The manual worker was machinist or stoker, or he worked at a conveyor-belt. The first result of this mechanization was a new degradation of labor, at least of manual labor, which now was clearly contrasted to "brain work."

Thus man has learned from his historical development that work gives shape and content to human existence and enables him to become more human. This is the anonymous and enduring experience of the farmer, and it is that of the free artisan in the town before the advent of technology. In our own day, we have become extremely conscious of the effect which labor has on the condition of man as man.

First of all, we have now a much more extensive view of mankind. In prehistory, and even today, we know of clans and tribes which live almost literally from hand to mouth. When we compare them with ourselves, we realize that civilized man by his work has not only transformed the face of the earth, but has also developed himself as a human being. He has discovered and exploited his own powers. This fact becomes particularly clear, when we see what is taking place in our own day. Today's experience teaches us much more than a study of primitive man.

The workman has progressed not only on the socioeconomic level, but also in the very work he is called to perform. Machines are constantly perfected and other machines are invented, as complements to them and to serve and control them. Man is thus progressing toward a position of lordship over a wholly automated plant. Work is becoming increasingly scientific. As a result there is a growing demand for educated workers. These workers realize that they, together with the administrative and technical directors, build up the industry. The contrast between classes, which became enormous under the impact of the technological revolution caused by the machine, is giving way to the unified work team that meets the revolution brought about by automation.

True, we are only on the way toward that lordly dominion. Innumerable workers have not yet a share in it. We see, however, how technology radically transforms the earth and ourselves. Today's old men, who were taught in their youth that the flying machine was impossible and now see the making and launching of rockets destined for the moon, are able to appreciate the distance man has traveled between then and now.

"Nature," "virgin nature," as Guardini remarks, has disappeared behind a "second nature," a nature of artificially created landscapes and synthetic raw materials. Man has become a technologically equipped nomad, roaming a megalopolis and even entire continents. Work has shaped the world and man, not only within the narrow dimensions in which farmers and townsmen formerly lived, but even unto the most distant lands and the most profound depths of his existence.

Thus it is not surprising that today's philosophy of labor is quite different from what it was formerly. Rather, that is the reason why such a philosophy is presently developing. Formerly labor was conceived as a precondition for the authentic kind of human existence, namely, contemplation in freedom from work. Today we see labor as a form of human life and of becoming man. Formerly, the adjectives "corporal" and "servile" were attached to the terms "labor" and "work," but we now connect these terms frequently with "human" and "liberating." Formerly, work was too frequently viewed as peripheral to human existence. Today it is found at the center. We can add that automation puts us on the road to a culture that will likewise be characterized by leisure.

In contrast to the Greek idea that labor is greatly inferior to contemplation, we now have the Marxist ideal of a world in which, though there is still room for other activities, everything is nonetheless ruled by labor and integrated in it. It is evident that, because of this shift in values, it is necessary that we specify our own position. This we shall try to do, beginning with some philosophical ideas. Here we gratefully borrow from modern experience and reflection.[2]

---

[2] We are greatly indebted here to S. Tellegen, "Wat is arbeid?" *Annalen v. h. Thijmgenootschap*, vol. 45 (1957), pp. 228-246; Remy C. Kwant, *Philosophy of Labor*, Pittsburgh, 1960; M. G. Plattel, "Wijsgerige beschouwingen rond het arbeidsbegrip," *Sociale Wetenschappen* (1957-58), pp. 149-161.

Labor means to make the earth subservient but also, through it, to liberate ourselves from nature, to give ourselves the freedom to be ourselves, to have dominion. Maurice Merleau-Ponty, the French philosopher, has well said: "History rests on labor, for labor is not a mere production of wealth; it is, more generally, the activity by which man projects around himself a human milieu and transcends what nature gives to his life." Remy C. Kwant justly adds that labor is the humanization of man through the humanization of the world.[3]

We can express this philosophical view in biblical terms by calling labor the fulfillment of the task given to man to "fill the earth and subdue it," as well as his self-realization as the image of God, for man is an image of Him precisely because he has "dominion over the fish of the sea, the birds of the air, the cattle, over all the wild animals and every creature that crawls on the earth."[4] Hence work should become a central category of our thinking about man. Our pastoral care, preaching and theology must always be orientated to, and seek to discover the questions that concern, man as realizing himself by means of his labor.

Only after we have made our own that broader and deeper vision and appreciation of labor, shall we be able to reflect properly on the limitations that are contained in that view. Labor has a central place. At the same time, however, it is not the whole of human existence. Work is a way to become man, but not every human self-realization is work.

On the contrary, he who maintains that every form of human self-realization is labor either says nothing at all or limits all value to labor. In the first alternative, his concept of work encompasses every human activity on earth and consequently says nothing about such relations as that between art and work, for instance, taking this term here in the narrow sense. In the second alternative, being a Marxist,

---

[3]Merleau-Ponty, "Autour du Marxisme," *Sens et Non-Sens*, 3rd. ed., n. d., p. 189. Kwant, *op. cit.*, pp. 3 f.
[4]Gen. 1, 27 ff.

he attributes no value to anything on earth except to the extent that it is concerned with labor. In this case, our earthly life is entirely encompassed by the process of production. Thus that which is central has in reality become supreme.

Against that idea, our Christian image of man, which is also authentically human, makes us state that there is something more in our earthly existence, a "plus" that cannot be reduced to productive labor. What is this "plus"? That is difficult to say, and for this reason we have not yet tried to give a definition of labor itself.

LABOR AND CULTURE

To describe this "plus," we could have recourse to the Greeks' contemplation—but what exactly is that? Is it solely an activity of the mind? Or has the body also a role in it and isn't labor also coupled with it? In general, isn't work involved in every form of human activity here below, whether it be art, or study, sport or feasting? Let us try nonetheless to find something in our existence that is the antipole of labor.

We shall never be able to find that antipole in a form of pure interiority. In all great cultures there have been men who strove for an ideal of "interiorization" and achieved it to a great extent. But it was never a pure interiorization. They strove for it by bodily exercises, by the recitation of consecrated formulae, by the contemplation of the faith that had been preached to them. Conversely, they made others share in the fruits of their own interiorization through teaching and spiritual help. They often pursued their interior life in the company of others, and according to a rule.

All this shows that man can never free himself entirely from his bodily being-in-the-world. It is possible that such a pure interiorization has nonetheless been desired and pursued under the influence especially of the Greek dualistic image of man. However, our modern concept of man makes us realize that *pure* interiority is fundamentally impossible and is therefore a false ideal. Man is a situated freedom and an intentional consciousness, an embodied spirit. He cannot escape from that nor should he try to escape from it.

It follows that, if we were to conceive contemplation as pure interiority and thus make it an antipole of labor, we would oppose a false ideal to the real task that is given to us. We would at the same time encourage the opinion that work is the be-all and end-all of human life.

We could draw the same conclusion from the scholastic distinction between transient and immanent action, between action that goes out of us and action that remains within us, when that distinction is used in the abstract. Scholastic philosophy names knowing and willing as the two directions of our immanent action. However, at least here on earth, there is never any pure knowing and pure willing, just as there is no purely spiritual soul. I know by means of sense perception and also by expressing and giving shape to things, by working. There exists a kind of thinking with our hands. And, in reverse, my work is also thoughtful, or at least conscious.

Concepts such as "contemplation" or "immanent activity," in their abstract formality, are therefore unsuitable as antipoles of work, for as such they would signify something that does not exist. But we can give those concepts a concrete, a fully human, content by integrating with them also exteriorization, embodiment, to the extent that these let man's interiority shine through and consciously express it. "Action," "transient action," or work, is then external action as intended in itself, hence directed to an outward effect, to a change of the world. Its opposite is then contemplation, not pure, but expressed and communicated in festive celebrations, in art and also in science.

With Plattel, we can similarly concretize the concept of "immanent action," which then implies expression and communication of that immanence. The outward activity is then

142

exercised to give expression to, and a share in, the content of the immanent action.

Using the terms of Kwant quoted above, we can say that man changes himself through his labor, but this change is implied in the changing of the world. Hence the antipole of labor is a change of the world, but with the intention of changing our human existence itself, or more generally with the intention of experiencing, expressing, and communicating this human existence. We could therefore call this antipole "communicating contemplation," "contemplative communion," the "production of, and communication in, *culture.*" For the sake of convenience, let us use the last term "culture," understood also actively as being occupied with the creation of culture, as the antipole of labor.

Labor and culture, then, differ in this that labor is the activity in which man aims at the world in order to change it, but culture is the activity in which man aims at himself in order to express and communicate himself. Work and the creation of culture differ therefore in their results. The result of labor is the *product,* which we can use in order to perfect our being-in-the-world. The result of culture is the *sign* in which our human existence expresses itself. However, the term "sign" is here taken in its broadest sense, as including both the sign that is a thing, and the sign that is an action. The product is *for* our fellow-man; it is at his service. The sign is directed *to* our fellow-man; it speaks to him. Hence labor is primarily the making of something, whereas the creating of culture is primarily to commune with someone. In labor, we subdue the earth. In culture, we go to our fellow-man, or at least make a sign which acts as a bridge to our fellow-man.

In formulating these descriptions, we based ourselves on the fact that there is no such thing as pure interiority or pure exteriority. But someone might now ask: Doesn't the same thing apply to those concepts of "labor" and "culture"? Our answer is that the same abstract formality *can* be contained in those concepts. There is no purely immanent activity, but on the other hand, are there activities which are nothing but expressions of an interiority? The "sign-thing" is always a product to some extent as well. Even a "sign-action" produces something, be it only a vibration in the air. That is why the creation of culture often shares greatly in the burdensome character of labor. There is no transmission of inspiration without perspiration. Conversely, man puts the stamp of his interiority on the products of his labor, and this is true also of his industrial labor.

That is why we can say, in the first instance, that the concepts "labor" and "culture," in the sense we have given to them, are both realized in human activity. They express, as we have said, two poles within every human activity. But those terms can also serve to designate two kinds of activity, in which case we distinguish them according to the predominance of one or the other of the two poles.

"Culture" is then the activity in which man expresses and communicates himself, whatever the amount of labor involved in the process. And "labor" is the productive activity, even when the sign value is not absent from it. This division almost coincides with the Church's juridical distinction between "liberal" and "servile" works, although the Greek value judgment must be removed from this distinction. Of course, the borderline between the two kinds is fluid. The "art industry" is a borderline case and so is scientific research. We hope, however, that this classification can help us to describe and delimit the human actions that constitute labor.

LABOR AND PLAY

Some may wonder why we did not name play as the antipole of labor. The principal reason is that it is extremely difficult to define play. Actually, we play without any preconceived purpose. That is why it is almost impossible to specify the finality, meaning, and content of our playing activities. Even among animals, certainly among the higher types, play begins to interrupt the rounds of useful activities. With us men, play constitutes its own world within the world of ordinary life. It has its own life amidst our "serious concerns," and as such has even a "seriousness" of its own.

Huizinga, after examining the various properties of play, summarizes them as follows: Play is "a free activity, in which we are aware of the fact that we don't mean it and that it is something outside ordinary life. Yet it can completely involve a player. No particular importance is attached to it, nor is any gain acquired by it. It takes place within a definite time and space. It is executed according to definite rules. It creates special social groups which like to surround themselves with mystery, or it accentuates its contrast with the ordinary world by make-up and disguise."[5]

Everything here points to something non-useful, non-purposive, non-obligatory, and non-forced. Karl Rahner, to our mind, has expressed the positive characteristics of play when he contrasts work with *musisch* activity—referring to both *Musze* (free time) and *Muse*—and then specifies this *musisch* activity further by saying that it is a self-realization of man in which he is not subject to the necessity of seeking to maintain himself against nature or by means of it.[6]

It is noteworthy that Rahner sees that self-realization of man as a free spirit precisely in that *"musisch"* activity, whereas Huizinga repeatedly stresses the fact that play is common to animals and men. And yet Huizinga also mentions freedom, and even calls animal play a manifestation of the spirit. Hence in the play of animals—we are speaking here only of higher animals—we can discern a foretoken of human play, so that the animal, and especially the higher animal, "foreshadows human existence" also in that respect.

---

[5] J. Huizinga *Homo ludens*, Haarlem, 1938, p. 20.
[6] Karl Rahner "Theologische Bemerkungen zum Problem der Freizeit," *Schriften zur Theologie*, IV, 1960, pp. 455-483. See also Pieper, *Leisure the Basis of Culture*, New York, 1952. However, the humanizing value of labor is hardly considered by Pieper. The difficulties of changing free time into genuine leisure are described very well by Sidney Lens, "A Shorter Work Week?" *The Commonweal*, Vol. LXXII, No. 5 (April 29, 1960) pp. 119-122.

Such non-complicated, useless and rather contentless play we observe also in primitive man and in children. All of us engage in it when we act in a primitive and childish fashion. But play also grows with the growth of man. Huizinga, if we understand him right, seems to look upon culture as a play that has acquired content, and in which human existence is no longer non-reflective but expresses itself thematically. This short digression may possibly be of some use to help us understand what work is.

Play is the most fundamental and essential antipole of work. In culture, play already mingles with work, and this cultural labor has a result. It produces a piece of work, and this characteristic precisely is absent from play. Let us add that play can also adopt the systematic organization of work, without aiming at a result that lies outside the play itself. This, we believe, is the case in sports. Work, on the contrary, is labor precisely to the extent that one does not linger in playful activity but keeps an eye on the result, on a product, on something that we can possess and enjoy throughout life.

Finally, work can also be described in contrast to "free time" but in that case there is different basis for the contrast. "Free time," or more specifically the activity with which we fill our free time, and which pragmatic moderns call "spending one's free time," is the antithesis of *professional* work, but it can also be cultural labor, or labor pure and simple, even though it is not done as part of one's job or profession. However, the fact that we so often contrast work with free time indicates that today work is strongly characterized as an exercise of one's function, as the fulfillment of a task.

MODERN LABOR

Having described labor more or less in a timeless fashion, we must now examine the characteristics of modern labor. This labor appears to us, first of all, as integrated into industry, that is, in machine production. Modern man no longer works in industry, or even in agriculture, with *tools* that are, as it were, extensions of his hands and that increase his bodily powers, but he works with *machines*. These are moved by some form of energy, and take over man's manual work in a largely independent way. We even have automated factories in which machines increasingly exercise the functions of regulation and control, because they are also taking over man's brain-work.

This mechanization gives today's human labor certain characteristics, some of which are temporary and others permanent. When the first steam engines appeared, man was truly called to "serve" them, to fire them or bring materials to them. The machine caused a lengthening of the working day and determined the tempo of work, which was later intentionally mechanized in the production line and conveyor belt. Since that time, various laws and collective contracts have given protection to the laborer, and much of the remaining heavy work has been taken over by the machine. Hence, at first the machine aggravated the burden of labor, but a further mechanization has practically done away with such burdens. The same can be said about the repetitious, impersonal, soul-killing character of labor. The human labor involved in attending to the conveyor belt has itself been taken over by machines, and control over these machines requires ever greater training. This does not mean that all heavy and impersonal work has disappeared. For one thing, in certain factories the machines have to run constantly and therefore require continous production.

Moreover, mechanization, or "scientification," as Kwant calls it, will continue to dominate all our work and increasingly so. Industrial work becomes more and more rationally divided into various functions and on that account requires increasingly specialized training. The same process is also at work outside industry, particularly in the realm of science. Hence, although work will not become impersonal in all fields, still man's full realization of his personal existence will shift to his leisure time. Leisure is gradually acquiring just as much importance as time-for-work in our human existence.

We said above that labor is a humanization of the world and that, precisely through this, it is also a humanization of man himself. We have sufficiently contrasted work to play and culture by indicating how the world is humanized through the production of things which can be used by man and which serve him. Our remarks concerning modern labor also emphasized the fact that man himself is undergoing a change. Modern man, in virtue of his labor, has attained a position of control over nature. At the same time, he is becoming more and more an employee and the bearer of a function within mankind. His position with respect to nature gives him undreamt-of possibilities for enriching his life. These possibilities are increasingly within the reach of the workmen themselves. The fact that more and more people continue to play a role in the process of work leads men to a new kind of fellowship, a new closeness of living together in cities and metropolitan areas. There is also a greater mobility, a kind of postagrarian nomadism. Unlike the pre-agrarian kind, however, this nomadism is not determined by the opportunities for hunting and cattle-breeding but by those for work and recreation. We hope to show later that, on account of that change, men are also in the process of forming a new image of the world, of man, and of God. For the time being we want to call attention to this new type of man which is developing throughout our western world and particularly within industry itself.

The Church, as we have said, must once more meet the workers, not only in their social struggle, but precisely in their human existence as laborers. This requires a reflective study of labor and a theology of labor. We cannot be satisfied with a few abstract theological remarks regarding the specific activity that constitutes labor. The world of labor and the type of man that is developing in it demand a theological scrutiny. We should like to trace here a few fundamental lines that could serve as a framework for such a reflective examination.

Labor and the World of Labor

In the preceding pages, we have described the place that labor actually occupies in our life. Today, everybody would agree that work, in one way or another, *must* find a place in our life. The Greek ideal of contemplation for the free man, which was based on the Greek image of man, is in that respect not so positive, especially with respect to manual labor. That is why we must be grateful that God's Revelation has come to us from a totally different human background. The Israelite was more inclined to cattle-breeding and agriculture than was the Greek city dweller. He had less aptitude for speculation and his idea or image of man did not prompt him to see anything contemptible in corporal work.

Hence man appears quite naturally as a working man in the canticle of praise of God as Creator which we find in Psalm 104. Here we read that "the beasts of the forest roam about . . . , young lions roar for the prey and seek their food from God. . . . , man goes forth to his work and to his tillage till the evening."[7] Labor is likewise implied in the first chapter of Genesis' story of creation, namely, in the commission given to man: "Fill the earth and subdue it."[8] In the sentence of condemnation, when man was expelled from the Paradise, work is presupposed rather than imposed.[9] Labor is also presupposed wherever death is shown as the cause of the fruitlessness of our work, particularly in Ecclesiastes,[10] and where God's blessing consists in the fruitfulness of labor.[11] The Commandment of the Sabbath also presupposes labor,[12] but work is apparently so normal that no particular commandment is formulated about it.

All this, of course, does not mean that there were no sluggards. Not without reason do the Sapiential books con-

---

[7]Ps. 104, 23.
[8]Gen. 1, 28.
[9]Gen. 3, 17-19.
[10]Eccles. 2, 18-23; 3, 9 ff.
[11]Ps. 127, 2; Is. 65, 20-23.
[12]Ex. 20, 9; Deut. 5, 13.

tain many proverbs condemning sloth.[13] Well-known is the saying: "Go to the ant, O sluggard, study her ways and learn wisdom . . . , she procures her food in summer."[14] On the other hand there is praise for the hard-working, worthy wife.[15]

Hence the ideal of industriousness, even of manual labor, is not left aside among the Jews for the sake of a more contemplative occupation. The monks of Qumran worked for their sustenance and the scribes had to know a trade.

This ethos of labor also animated the men of the New Testament. First of all, Our Lord Himself. He chose to grow up in the family of a carpenter.[16] In Nazareth He Himself was a carpenter.[17] His parables often suggest His contact with working people in His surroundings, particularly fishermen and farmers. We also see, now and then, in the Gospels that preaching itself was hard work; for instance, when Jesus had not time to eat,[18] or when He was tired and sat down near a well.[19]

Christ thus fulfilled the work which the Father had given Him, and this He did throughout life or, in His own words recorded by St. John, "while it is day."[20] For, "my food is to do the will of Him who sent me, to accomplish His work."[21] It is striking also that, on the human level, He remained within the frame of a function, namely, that of rabbi. Personally, I have been struck by the fact that the Son of God chose to follow the pattern of work that was well known

[13]Prov. 6, 6-11; 10, 26; 13, 4; 15, 19; 18, 9; 19, 24; 20, 4; 21, 25; 22, 13; 24, 30-34; 26, 13-16; Eccl. 22, 1 ff.
[14]Prov. 6, 6.
[15]Prov. 31, 10-31: "She obtains wool and flax and makes cloth with skillful hand . . . , she picks out a field to purchase; out of her earnings she plants a vineyard. She is girt about with strength and sturdy are her arms . . . ; she puts her hands to the distaff and her fingers ply the spindle."
[16]Matt. 13, 55.
[17]Mark 6, 13: "Is not this the carpenter, the son of Mary?"
[18]Mark 3, 20 "And they could not so much as take their food."
[19]"Jesus, wearied as he was from the journey, was sitting at the well." John 4, 6.
[20]John 9, 4.
[21]John 4, 34.

in His time, that of the itinerant rabbi.[22] Throughout His earthly life both hidden and public, He, the most original of all men, wished to stay within the framework of human existence proper to His time and to take part in the functions pertaining to the society of His days.

The same must be said of Christ's Apostles. Most of the Twelve were fishermen. They knew the arduous work of their occupation, even to the extent of laboring in vain a whole night.[23] Their association with Christ implied a sharing in His burdensome task. In the administration of the Church, they manifest that they had assumed a well-defined task: "We will devote ourselves to prayer and to the ministry of the word."[24]

The burden and task of an Apostle is most clearly seen in the life of him whom the Risen Christ personally called to that function, the "least of the apostles," who nevertheless "labored more than any of them."[25] St. Paul stands closer to us moderns than anyone else in the New Testament. Perhaps he stands even closest to the modern worker, for he plied a trade and at the same time shared fully in the international culture of his time. No doubt, his chief task was the apostolate and in particular that of a missionary. He realized that he was called not to administer the sacraments, but to "preach the gospel."[26]

We learn how much labor and care that apostolic work entailed from St. Paul's pathetic description which he saw himself forced to give, on account of the attacks of his enemies.[27] In addition to that burdensome work of evangelization, he labored with his hands and applied himself to mental pursuits. In contrast to most Christian preachers, whose right St. Paul acknowledges, he did not wish to be a burden

---

[22]Cf. P. Schoonenberg, *Het galoof van ons doopsel.* Vol. I, pp. 114 f.
[23]"The whole night through we have toiled and have taken nothing" Luke 5, 5; John 21, 3.
[24]Acts 6, 4.
[25]1 Cor. 15, 9, 11.
[26]1 Cor. 1, 17.
[27]2 Cor. 6, 3-10; 11, 22-29.

to any community, but to a great extent took care of his personal needs by plying the trade of tentmaker.[28] He cared not only for his own financial needs and those of his companions,[29] but also tried to help the needy brethren of Jerusalem.[30] Yet he remained, as one commentator has called him, a "typical intellectual." He was in his own time what today we would call a trained theologian and this he remained in his apostolic work.

St. Paul had studied in the "school" of Gamaliel in Jerusalem, the theological center of the most orthodox form of Judaism. He made his own an enormous amount of knowledge of the Old Testament and of Jewish thought. Hence his great letters contain also a first confrontation of the Christian message with the Old Testament and Jewish exegesis. For this reason, this tentmaker, outdoor preacher and instructor was at the same time the first Christian theologian.

It should not surprise us therefore that this workman and his associates have some scornful words to brand the sloth of Athenians and Cretans.[31] His own example gives him every right to urge Christians to work, when such an admonition is necessary. Writing to the Ephesians, he says:[32] "He who was wont to steal, let him steal no longer, but rather let him labor, working with his hands at what is good." And he adds: "that he may have something to share with him who suffers need," where others might have been satisfied with saying, "that he may earn his living."

We recognize here the Apostle who did not want to be a burden to others, but wished to live according to Christ's words, "It is more blessed to give than to receive."[33] St. Paul formulates most explicitly the obligation of work, adding his own conduct as a motive, against those who did not labor,

[28]Acts 18, 3; 20, 34; 1 Thess. 3, 8 f; 1 Cor. 9, 4-18; 2 Cor. 12, 13.
[29]Acts 20, 34.
[30]Gal. 2, 10; 1 Cor. 16, 1-4; 2 Cor. 8 and 9.
[31]"Cretans, always liars, evil beasts, lazy gluttons" Tit. 1, 12; "Now all the Athenians and the visitors there from abroad used to spend all their leisure telling or listening to something new" Acts 17, 21.
[32]Eph. 4, 28.
[33]Acts 20, 25.

apparently in order to be free for what they called spiritual service, or perhaps in order to be prepared for the coming of the Lord—for the passage is contained in a letter which corrects wrong eschatological expectations:

> And we charge you, brethren, in the name of our Lord Jesus Christ, to withdraw yourselves from every brother who lives irregularly, and not according to the teaching received from us. For you yourselves know how you ought to imitate us; for we were not unruly while with you, neither did we eat any man's bread at his cost, but we worked night and day in labor and toil, so that we might not burden any of you. Not that we did not have the right to do so, but that we might make ourselves an example for you to imitate us. For indeed when we were with you we used to charge you: if any man will not work, neither let him eat. For we have heard that some among you are living irregularly, doing no work but busy at meddling. Now such persons we charge and exhort in the Lord Jesus Christ that they work quietly and eat their own bread.

> But you, brethren, do not grow tired of well-doing. And if anyone does not obey our word by this letter, note that man and do not associate with him, that he may be put to shame. Yet do not regard him as an enemy, but admonish him as a brother.[34]

Accordingly, from its inception Christianity brought with it an ethos of labor, and it has to a great extent remained faithful to it. The teaching and especially the example of St. Paul have been very important in that respect. St. John Chrysostom and many others were inspired by it and they pointed out the nobility of manual labor to the great and the rich of the ancient pagan world.[35]

The monks likewise thought they were obliged to do manual labor in imitation of St. Paul, and this they were taught by St. Basil, St. Augustine and St. Benedict. The opposite view was held by St. Thomas Aquinas in his de-

---

[34] 2 Thess. 3, 6-15.
[35] Hom. 1 in Illud: *Salutate Priscillam et Aquilam*, 5, MG 51, 193-196.

fense of the mendicant Orders.[36]   The monks were also the great teachers of labor for the Germanic peoples.

All this, however, hardly answers the question as to why work must play so great a role in the life of the Christian and of man. Undoubtedly, the Church has increased the esteem of the worker in ancient times, that is, the slave. She herself has taught and practiced labor through her monks. She has richly blessed the trade organization of the medieval guilds. She has, albeit belatedly and distantly, defended the rights of the working class. But there has scarcely been any reflections upon the nature of labor in the light of Faith. As we have said already, it is only in our own day that a theology of labor begins to be formulated. We realize better the difficulty of such a task, when we keep in mind that Scripture and Tradition offer only scattered materials for such a theology. The principal interest of Christian preaching lay elsewhere. Instead of bewailing this fact, we now should like to indicate a few lines according to which such a theology could be constructed.

LABOR AND MAN

Man is a creature who received the task to be himself and to bring about his own full realization. This task implies that he must free himself from nature and make it serve him through his labor. This idea is equivalently in the mind of the writer of the first chapter of Genesis, when he makes God say:

> Let us make mankind in our image and likeness; and let them have dominion over the fish of the sea, the birds of the air, the cattle, over all the wild animals and every creature that crawls on the earth.[37]

---

[36]St. Basil, *Regulae fusius tractatae*, 37-42, MG 31, 1009-1027; St. Augustine: *De opere monachorum*, ML 40, 547-582; St. Benedict, *Regula*, c. 48, ML 16, 713 f; S. Thomas Aquinas, *Summa Theologica*, p. 2-2ae, q. 187, a 3. Pope Pius XII recommended manual labor or intellectual work to contemplative cloistered Sisters in his Constitution "Sponsa Christi," *Acta Apostolicae Sedis,* vol 18. (1951), 13 ff.

[37]Gen. 1, 26.

And then, speaking to man:

> Be fruitful and multiply; fill the earth and subdue it.
> Have dominion over the fish of the sea, the birds of the
> air, the cattle, and all the animals that crawl on the
> earth.[38]

In these terms "dominion" and "subduing," work is
merely implied. The kind of labor which the writer had in
mind appears to have been rather primitive, for he always
refers to the animal world as its object. This text, which
belongs to the priestly tradition of the Pentateuch, is rather
a hieratic remembrance of the patriarchal era than a pro-
gram for labor in the Israel of the author's time, and still
less for our own time. The same can be said about the texts
concerning the Sabbath.[39] Only incidentally does the immediate human motive of rest and freedom make itself felt
in such texts.[40]

They show us, nevertheless, that work is conceived as belonging to human existence, and at the same time that it is not
the totality of this existence. Hence, basing ourselves on
Scripture, we are permitted to call labor a task that flows
from man's nature. We must now examine this task further
and especially determine how it must be executed.

There exists, then, a *duty* of labor, and we have seen how
this duty is emphasized by St. Paul. It is a duty every man
has toward himself, namely, to realize himself through work.
It is even more a duty toward others. The Apostle states
this in the popular rule: "If any man will not work, neither
let him eat."[41] He who wishes to live by the fruit of another
man's labor must take a share in labor. And "labor," cer-
taintly in our own day, must be taken here in its widest sense.

The unemployment that is caused by the shifts in today's
process of production, and which we must expect to reappear
over and over again, has led to the idea of a *right* to work.

[38]Gen. 1, 28.
[39]Gen. 2, 2 f.; Ex. 16, 22-30; Ex. 20, 8-11; Deut. 5, 12-15.
[40]Ex. 23, 13; Deut. 6, 14 f.
[41]2 Thess. 3, 10.

It is certain that everyone has a duty of charity to help the unemployed in the measure of possibility and that the best kind of help consists in giving people an opportunity for work. To the extent that such a duty acquires a concrete shape in a community, there will also appear a definite right of those who are unemployed. Such a right is also possessed by those who are partially incapacitated.

Much more evident is the right of a worker to decent working conditions, as also his duty to respect the property of the employer. Of course, it is not the function of a theology of labor to work out those rights and duties in detail. That is why we shall now speak about man's fellow-man, to the extent that labor itself is directed to him.

The task to "subdue the earth" is preceded by another: "Be fruitful and multiply."[42] When cultivating the world, man is variously directed toward his fellow-man. He is oriented toward those who work with him and also toward those for whom the fruits of his labor are destined. These relations have been immeasurably increased in our modern organization of labor. Instead of the family as a community of labor, which is still somewhat preserved among farmers, there are groups of workers in factories, stores, and offices. These experience a certain bond arising from their work. This bond, which is one of the characteristic phenomena of our time, may be called "fellowship." It is usually restricted to laborers in the narrow sense of the word, despite all the differences existing between skilled and unskilled laborers. The bond is perhaps beginning to show a tendency to include also managing personnel, but it certainly includes also the workers in other trades and in other countries.

The closeness of that sort of community grows to the extent that labor not only demands mutual respect and care, but also the combination of each one's contribution to the same teamwork.

The products of labor also find ever larger, international, and world-wide markets. Industries become interdependent

---

[42]Gen. 1, 28.

with respect to their products, so that even the fruits of men's labors are instrumental in creating solidarity in the world of workers and in the whole of mankind. Moreover, a large section of the working class, those engaged in transportation and communication, are directly in the service of man's encounter with his fellow-men, whatever its nature may be.

Finally, to the extent that work develops man himself, it makes him also more ready and eager for contact with others. That is why we observe today that the worker does not confine himself to relations with his fellow-worker, whether near or far, who shares his particular interests. He manifests a desire to share and meet the culture of other countries and peoples. This can hardly be explained solely by the greater facilities of travel and by the fact that he can own a television set. He wants these things because he already has a longing for such contacts.

In spite of all, however, labor remains first of all the humanization of the world. It does not primarily aim to promote more social relations with one's fellow-man. No matter how much influence work exercises today on human society and culture, we notice also that it is more and more divorced from the rest of life. Industrial work is done behind the walls of a factory. Between man's youth and his labor there lies a period of schooling and training. The whole system of relations and functions has become so involved that the adolescent is often on the defensive against it or is indifferent, and his maturity is thereby delayed.

Moreover, relations within the world of labor itself are not those in which persons become involved with one another in their innermost being. They are functional associations. Although the fellowship between workers can transcend purely material interests, it is not friendship. There might even be signs of the opposite. For all these reasons, we must once again focus our attention on two things: the kinds of activity which are necessary besides labor in order that man may lead a truly human life with his fellow-men, and, secondly, the possibilities, within labor itself, of pursuing that social life.

Theoretically speaking, all agree that there should be leisure for man's social existence through culture, play, friendly gatherings, etc. In practice, the rationalization of labor through technology has also made more leisure time available for nearly everybody. Technology provides an abundance of means for occupying that free time. To what extent our technological civilization threatens once more to dehumanize this free time is a question that would deserve a special chapter.

In connection with work, Catholic teaching should draw attention to the need for life together with our fellow-men over and above professional relationships. Perhaps we shall thereby contribute to forming men who are not only breadwinners but also true fathers of families. Juvenile delinquency, according to American experience, seems to be fostered when the father is only a breadwinner. We should also stress the value of family life as such, whatever form this life may adopt in the future. Now that the family has lost almost all its functions, on account of technological labor, it has become so much more irreplaceable as a community of persons.

Apart from the danger contained in the absence of the father, there is now also that of the absence of the mother. We cannot proclaim a clear-cut "Catholic doctrine" concerning the situation in which married women have jobs outside the home—although such claims have been frequently made in the past. However, we can indicate principles and cultivate an attitude that will enable the coming generation to seek and find an answer.

The work of a married woman can have advantages even for marriage itself. The working wife is more of a help and an understanding companion to the husband than is the wife who is kept at home as an immature luxury doll. That is why the work of the wife is stimulated not only by economic factors but also by an ever increasing equality between man and woman even within marriage itself. On the other hand, there is at least one danger connected with such work, namely, the absence of the mother from the home. The children who, in various countries of Europe and America, return home at night from the day nursery and meet a tired mother and father, should serve as a warning.

Relationships with our fellow-man, apart from professional bonds, should be promoted, but such relations should not be entirely absent from labor either. Work itself is a service in and for the love of our fellow-man. Its explicit function and particular characteristic, however, is that of exercising dominion over the world. Is there room for that service of love within the exercise of dominion?

One can, of course, have the intention of doing his work as a service of love. In our day, however, "intention" or "purpose" have the connotation of something that is "imposed," that is "brought in from outside." Let us therefore begin by establishing the fact that there can also be an intention in man's life which coincides with the inner structure of what he is doing. Thus, for example, we can offer up to God our work of building family dwellings not for the conversion of Thibet but for the families that will occupy those houses. Such an intention would indicate that we consecrate ourselves as human beings and Christians to the work we are performing and to the human beings for whom we are doing it. However, such an intention will remain more or less abstract if it is not really experienced, if it is not a part of a *mystique* of labor. Perhaps it is sometimes possible to reach such a condition on the human level. No doubt, the work in which man enters into functional relation with his fellow-men, in stores, for example, or at the ticket-window, provides good, though often difficult, occasions for serving one's neighbor in a loving way within the realm of business relations with him. In respect to other forms of labor, is it not possible that workers will realize more and more the significance of their products for people all over the world, through their personal contact with consumers or through news coverage of nearby and distant lands which benefit from the fruits of their labors? The industrial enterprise itself can give instruction and information that will make the workers more conscious of their considerable contribution for good. The burden of labor can then be borne, not only in virtue of a rationally formed intention, but with a joyful realization of the concrete way in which workers benefit human beings outside the walls of the factory.

But mankind is also present within the factory itself. Hence there should be genuine fellowship and the cultivation of authentic human relations by the management. This demands that the latter be animated by genuine human concern and not simply by the desire to make human machines more productive. If that concern is present, it also can contribute toward making the worker realize that he is a fellow human being. All this would remain within the context of work itself.

LABOR AND GOD

The expression "mystique of labor," which we have just used, is more appropriate when we consider labor in its relation to God. Let us first examine this relationship insofar as it arises from us as creatures in reference to God our Creator. This is an aspect that continues to exist in our supernatural relation to God, and it is of fundamental importance for labor, which is essentially a natural human activity. The fact that we have been raised to the supernatural order affects labor also, but it does not change its place in creation.

God gave man the task of subduing the earth.[43] To work is to obey that command. It is therefore a service of God, a loving service. Of course, this must not be understood in the sense that God imposed a positive obligation upon man from without or arbitrarily added an accidental destiny to human life. The duty to work comes from God by the fact that our whole being comes from Him. It can be useful to urge man to work by appealing to God's will. When we address ourselves to modern man, however, we must always make him realize also that God's will is expressed in our very nature.

---

[43]Gen. 1, 28.

160

Here also, as in all the rest of our ethics, it is necessary to substitute for the appeal to divine commands the understanding of what is demanded by our created nature and by its supernatural privileges. God wills our labor, because work belongs to the very life and existence of man. Because this point has been sufficiently explained above, we may now offer a contribution to a mystique of labor by examining labor in reference to God's creative activity.

Let us recall, first of all, that Scripture pictures God's creative activity itself as a work, namely that of a potter. This figure is used, for example, when He forms children in the womb, and fashions man out of dust.[44] God's work, however, is also represented as an ordering by His word. As we read repeatedly in the first chapter of Genesis, "God said and so it was." Moreover, God's activity is frequently shown as God's exercise of dominion over man and the world, over nature and history. The writer of that first chapter sees in man an image of that dominion. Dominion over all animals is what he gives immediately as explanation for man's being made after the image of God. Just as we have shown that man's work is implied in this dominion, so we can also see in this dominion of man a sign that he is an image of the Creator.

Man as a maker is an image of God as Creator. God creates out of nothing. Human making also is the production of something new and, to that extent, also out of nothing, especially insofar as technical labor is concerned. God creates completely from nothing. Neither matter nor form are presupposed by His creation. As the classical formula expresses it, God creates *"ex nihilo sui et subjecti."* Man, on the contrary, "creates" only in the sense that he gives a new form to pre-existing matter. He makes something only *"ex nihilo sui"*; the new thing he makes was not there before. But in doing this, man can be very "creative," especially today when technical products are so far above the raw materials of nature.

---

[44]E.g., Gen. 2, 7; Job 10, 8-11.

161

Man, nevertheless, remains dependent on nature. That is why all his labor, even when it is technical, is a laborious struggle, in contrast to God's powerful word as recorded in the first chapter of Genesis. Man, while experiencing a legitimate pride in his "creations," can perhaps learn humility from his burdensome struggles when he compares them to God's creation.

Labor is thus both image of and contrast to God's creative activity, but it is also integrated in the latter. For God not only has created, but continues to create. Genesis says that He rested on the seventh day, but, according to the word of Our Lord, in that rest "My Father works even until now."[45] There is not only God's majestic work "in the beginning," as described in the first chapter of Genesis, but there are other texts, such as Psalm 103 and Job 38-40, which describe God's continued activity. The world is continually sustained by the word of His power, and all being and activity in the world are worked by God Himself. God is not a "retired engineer." He is the One by whom and "in whom we live and move and are."[46]

This point, it seems to us, is the most important thing we can say about God in reference to our work. Here we should correct the concept we spontaneously form of this relationship. According to this concept, God has made nature only to the extent that nature has not been the object of our labor. This nature, we may add, is almost concealed behind the "second" nature produced by man's work, or exists only as a kind of "natural reserve" not yet touched by man. We easily think that, after God had finished making nature, *we* took over and we work, but God rests.

To this we reply that God is equally operative in man's own works. Our labor does not make His work superfluous, for God fulfills and realizes our work and makes us do it. Hence we should remember that He is present and at work in all our works. This consideration is the more necessary

[45]John 5, 17.
[46]Acts 17, 28.

today, because modern man takes over the works that were formerly thought to be reserved to God. We must not imagine God as a worker among the men and things that operate in this world. He transcends them and hence is all in all. God is at work in the growth of plants. He is equally at work in them when we foster their growth by artificial fertilizers. He is present once more in the fabrication of the most synthetic of all fertilizers. Our work likewise does not take anything out of God's hands, for He supports it together with our whole existence.

In spite of all that, our work remains "profane." And here we meet again the same limitation as in our preceding discussions. Labor is not the whole of man's activity. Hence it cannot make man live to the fullness of his human existence. It cannot make him experience his whole relationship to his fellow-men and his whole relationship to God. Since work is primarily directed to the earth which it subdues or to the product which it creates, it is not the complete sign of what we are, in relation to ourselves, our fellow-men, and God. Labor is a service of God, but not a religious service in the narrow sense of the term, and certainly not worship. It is this precisely that we intend, neither more nor less, when we call labor "profane."

This term does not mean that labor is tarnished or desecrated, profane in a primitive sense, as if it really ought not to be so. Labor is profane in a purely negative sense. It is not sacral nor ought it to be, for that is not its nature. Hence "profane" does not mean without relation to God, but it means without express and explicit relation to God, in contrast to "sacral," which has precisely an express relation to God. "Profane" and "sacral," then, give us primarily not a division of men or things, but of human activities, and divide men or things only to the extent that they are involved in these activities.

The profane and the sacral exist only because we give meaning to things. An activity is sacral when our attitude toward God is signified in preaching, in a holy celebration, in prayer and the like. Sacral actions belong to the signifying activity in which man communicates his interior dispositions to others; i.e., to the category of human activity which we have opposed to labor in our previous discussion. Labor, then, is profane by its very nature. The sacral can come close to it, for example, in the blessing of a workshop or factory, but it can never essentially transform work. That is why we can repeat about the relation of labor to God what we said about its relation to man and fellow-man: our attitude to God must be signified in a sacral way *alongside* our labor, and the sacral can be lived only *implicitly* in our work.

The sacral must have its place alongside labor. This must be so, first of all, on Sundays. Today we must defend Sunday against a threat on the part of labor itself, but also against the growing tendency to devote all leisure to profane pursuits. This point can bring a return to what constitutes the core of the Christian celebration of Sunday.

The celebration of Sunday does not consist fundamentally in rest, as was, broadly speaking, the case of the Sabbath ("rest") in the Old Testament, but it consists essentially in the celebration of the Eucharist. The early church knew only the latter during the era of persecutions. Later, rest from labor was slowly added again to the celebration of Sunday.

Rest from work has great social advantages, and yet this should not be the Church's first concern, for the State has the authority and the means to insure that. The Church's task is to provide a suitable time and place for the Eucharistic celebration. This idea suggests that Catholics should not adopt too severe and formal a concept of the Sunday rest, such as may have inspired Protestant thinking in the past and also the "Blue Laws" in the United States. On the other hand, we could learn a lesson from Protestant brethren, who combat the massive use of the Sunday for sports events, insofar as this use tends to change the Lord's Day into a sports day.

In this matter also, our religious teaching must, first of all, try to form a mentality that will guide the conduct of future generations of Christians in their new situations. This applies notably to the desire expressed from time to time by industry to introduce the "sliding work week." It is not too difficult to imagine that one who celebrates the Lord's Day on his own free day within such a sliding work week will find more restful surroundings on such a day than on present Sundays in the summer, with their massive migrations to and from the countryside and sports parks. On the other hand, efforts must be made to promote the celebration of the Holy Eucharist within the parochial community and especially to have the family celebrate it together. For the present, one does not see how this can be achieved otherwise than by keeping Sunday as a day of rest for all. We shall not discuss this matter further, for the theology of Sunday requires a chapter by itself.

There still remains the question whether work, though characterized as profane, is nevertheless experienced implicitly as a service of God. Here again, as when we spoke of labor as a service of our fellow-man, we are not thinking of an intention we could only mentally form, but of a *mystique*. Is a "mystique of labor" possible through which labor brings us in contact not only with our fellow-man but also with God? The answer depends on the worker himself, and even more so in this respect than in regard to man's social relations. All we can say here is "perhaps." Perhaps men will become more keenly aware of the fact that God is at work in their labor and that their products are His creation, as we have explained above. Perhaps man's experience and his conscious acceptance of the limits which nature imposes on him, because of the things it offers, will awaken and foster that religious awareness and attitude. Perhaps the *mystique* of serving our fellow-man through labor can also be animated and inspired, at least as far as the Christian worker is concerned, by Christ's word "what you have done to the least of my brethren you have done to Me."[47] We can say only "this is what we hope for."

---

[47]Matt. *25,* 40.

Later we shall speak of labor in connection with sin and salvation. Then we shall see that only the salvation brought by Christ has made it possible for us sinful men to find not only God, but ourselves and our fellow-man, in and through our labor. The Christian worker will perhaps find in this idea an element of his *mystique* of labor in the sense we have given to it.

It is useful to underscore once more that labor, though profane and natural, is taken up in a supernatural order and is directed to a supernatural end. Labor makes this world a better world for the children of God, for our brothers and sisters in Christ. It makes this earth a more suitable road to heaven. In fact, it prepares the new heaven and the new earth in which justice will reign.[48] By the fact that it is directed to our supernatural life and that this life carries our labor, we can call it not only the humanization of the world but a "consecration." This expression of Rideau was used also by Pius XII, though only in a passing way, in his discourse to the Second World Congress of the Lay Apostolate.[49]

Later we shall try to determine more precisely to what extent work, as part of our human existence, does prepare that final situation and how it does consecrate the present world.

In any case, we must emphasize the fact that labor stands *within* and not outside our supernatural life, and conversely that we are Christians and ascend to the final kingdom of God not merely in connection with, but *in* our labor. We can try to express this idea by reflecting on the terms "profession" and "vocation." Catholics use the latter term almost exclusively for the priestly or religious state. We should realize, however, that our first vocation is that of living in Christ. This vocation has its source in God's predestination and ends in justification and sanctification.[50]

---

[48]"We look for new heavens and a new earth, according to his promises, wherein dwells justice." 2 Peter 3, 13.

[49]*Acta Apostolicae Sedis*, Vol. 24, (1957), p. 927.

[50]"And those whom he has predestined, them he has also called, and . . . has also justified, and . . . also glorified." Rom. 8, 30.

That is why St. Paul's letters are so often addressed to those who "are called to be saints."[51] All other vocations are special forms of that fundamental vocation:[52] that of a priest, of virginal union with the Lord, but likewise also any other kind of Christian life. They are all vocations and a gift of grace, a "charism."[53]

Can we say the same of a profession? It is certain that a "vocation" is more totally human. We speak more readily of the vocation of a father of a family than of the vocation of a tailor, of that of a priest than of the vocation of a theologian. However, just as labor is central in human existence—but at the same time is not the whole of life nor governs life entirely—so can a profession occupy a central place in our vocation. It can be an important embodiment of our vocation, namely, that of being a Christian in the world.

We have now sketched to some extent what our natural and supernatural relations to God signify for our work. Conversely, our work is also significant for our life for God, as is true of our whole human existence. It is possible to look upon modern labor principally as constituting a danger for man's religious life. This it is *also*. Not only is it a threat to our Christian Sunday, but also to our prayer and finally to our apostolic work. It can lead to haste and restlessness.

However, we priests should not put too much blame on the "modern world." The world has often hidden partners, such as a neurotic activism that prompts us to hurry and shorten our prayers, that makes us perform apostolic functions as if we were standing at a conveyor-belt. There is especially the depersonalized tempo of our Holy Mass and our administration of the sacraments. We should, then, not overrate the real danger that comes to us from the world of labor.

Moreover, we must also realize that this world offers positive opportunities and tasks, even in respect to religious life

[51]For example, Rom. 1, 7.
[52]"Paul, the servant of Jesus Christ, called to be an apostle." Rom. 1, 1.
[53]Cf. 1 Cor. 7, 7: "Each one has his own gift from God, one in this way, and another in that."

itself. Thus the fact that our tempo of work increasingly makes pure meditative prayer more difficult can also make us rediscover the centuries-old *lectio divina,* the prayerful reading of Holy Scripture. But, above all, our world of labor can be an invitation to a new understanding of what God wants to be for us. Let us say a few words about that.

In a world which he controls and dominates only to a very small extent, man can look upon God from the standpoint of nature and represent Him as being principally active in the fields that are most beyond his dominion. God created in the beginning. He gives fruitfulness where man has worked the soil. He cures the illnesses for which man has not yet any remedies. He restrains the power of our enemies. But the natural sciences reveal more and more the earthly causes that are at work in these realms. They even accept the principle that every phenomenon has an immanent cause within this world, and technical labor gives us an ever increasing control over those causes. In this way God seems to disappear from the world. The prayer "give us this day our daily bread" seems to have become superfluous.

One could now say that God gives us understanding, power, courage and love, in order to enable us to subdue and rule over the world. Even in this respect, however, we discover and learn to control more and more factors that are physically operative. We must therefore realize that, with respect to both the outside world and our entire self, God does not operate in order to take the place of the world's immanent causes or to complete them. He does not intervene and make Himself a cause on the same level as other causes. God stands above them all, as the independent, transcendent God, who continues to create all things.

Is there, then, no relation between Himself and each individual person, is there no love of election by which He calls every one by his own name? Yes, there is. However, this love does not concern His work of creation, but rather man's elevation to the supernatural order, which is not a work but a giving of Self. We can subdue the earth with courage and love, because He is our God and Father, even as the Hebrews were freed from Egyptian bondage, not because God stood with them on a battle-chariot, but because He lived in them and His presence gave them power.

Today we understand God's transcendence better, because of our dominion over the world through our labor. Our prayer now seeks first to obtain God's supernatural presence. This presence, moreover, is precisely the reason for our faith and our ability to pray. Now that we are able to manufacture our own food, we have every reason to interpret the prayer for our daily bread as connected with that for the coming of the Kingdom which is God's self-giving in Christ. We can pray the Our Father best in celebrating the Holy Eucharist, which is thanksgiving because the kingdom has already come to us.

LABOR AND SIN

Christianity, as we have already remarked, is always coupled with an ethos of labor, but until our own day it has not produced any theology of labor. Three factors seem to have acted as the principal obstacles in that respect. The first is the unworldliness of Christianity. This was particularly evident in the first centuries, when Christians looked forward with eager expectation to the new heaven and the new earth. There is an echo of this mentality in the liturgy and mysticism, especially in the Eastern Church. The Western Church has lived more closely to earthly reality, as is evident from what we have said regarding her relations with the world of labor.

There are two other factors that have prevented the growth of a theology of labor, namely, St. Augustine's view of original sin and the absence of a *philosophy* of labor within the Church. We have tried to neutralize the latter factor somewhat in what we have said above. Hence we can now give our attention to the influence of the doctrines regarding the original sin and man's last things.

169

In this matter, it is not at all necessary to tone down Revelation regarding these points. When we look at the nature of sin, we see it as a fact belonging to the moral-religious order. Hence the person—but not nature—is seen to be touched by it, so that salvation refers to the same sphere. When eschatology promises us a final community of love, in which God is all in all, then everything that brings about the realization of our human existence and community on earth, hence also labor, is related to it. Let us develop this consideration by successively confronting work with sin, salvation, and man's final fulfillment.

We have given sufficient thought to the place of labor in the life of man, in his relations with his fellow-man and with God, as a creature and adopted son, but we did not mention the Fall of man. We were justified in leaving this point out, for labor did not enter the world as a consequence of sin. The scriptural words about thistles and thorns and the sweat of man's brow, which are so often mentioned in our religious teaching concerning work, as well as the view that work is penitential, must not make us forget that labor belongs to the very existence of man.

Scripture itself expresses this clearly enough. God's command to "subdue the earth" in Genesis' first story of creation (Ch. 1) does not mention sin.[54] In Genesis 3, 17-19, nothing more is said than that work will be more difficult from then on. Labor itself is also presupposed in the story of Eden and the Fall. We read in Chapter Two of Genesis[55]: "The Lord God took the man and placed him in the garden of Eden *to till it and to keep it.*" Even though there is some doubt regarding the accuracy of that translation, we can point to the meaning labor has in reference to nature, which is so wonderfully expressed in the preceding lines of the same chapter: "There was not yet any field shrub on the earth nor had the plants of the field sprung up, *for* the Lord God had sent no rain on the earth and *there was*

[54]Gen. 1, 28.
[55]Gen. 2, 15.

no man to till the soil."[56] Work owes its existence and
meaning to God's creative activity. The curse that rests
upon it is due to sin. Labor is given with human existence,
but because of sin it has become more burdensome, like the
rest of human existence.

On the basis of that story of Eden and through the influence of St. Augustine, numerous generations have thought
that human nature, though not essentially changed, was im-
paired by the sin of him who was chronologically the first
man. He made us lose this nature's preternatural perfection.
Through his sin death and illness, deterioration and tired-
ness invaded mankind.

Today there is a great change in that view of man, so much
so that the entire doctrine concerning original sin seems to
be affected. As we have explained elsewhere,[57] in our opinion
it is possible to have another view of man than that of St.
Augustine without going beyond the boundaries imposed by
that dogma. We shall therefore limit ourselves here to two
remarks.

First of all, we believe that the Fall can be conceived as a
history of personal sins, which in their interconnection have
shut off mankind's access to God's grace—unless the gates
are reopened by Christ as Savior. Secondly, the Fall exercises
its influence in the personal sphere and introduces changes in
the significance the body and the world have for us, but it
does not affect their physical structure. However, the last
observation needs to be made with reservations in view of
the words of the Synod of Carthage[58] concerning the death of
the body as a punishment for Adam's Fall. Does that statement oblige us to hold that a real change occurred in human
nature? If so, the essential role of a single ancestor is obvious
and we must at least in part accept St. Augustine's view. We
leave unsolved the question whether our two remarks are

---

[56]Gen. 2, 5.
[57]P. Schoonenberg, *Het geloof van ons doopsel,* vol. IV, 's Hertogenbosch, 1962, pp. 73-200. The matter is more fully developed
in our article: "Natuur en zondeval," *Tijdschrift voor Theologie,* vol. 2
(1962), pp. 173-200.
[58]Denzinger, No. 101.

valid without any reservation. Hence we do not develop those ideas for the whole of human life. We believe, however, that we can safely use them as a starting point for an explanation of what labor has become since sin entered the world.

We think, therefore, that neither the earth nor man's muscles have been changed by sin and even that the unity of his body and spiritual personality has not been changed either. What has been changed, we think, is man's personal attitude toward work.

When man stands outside the Covenant with God who is his Rock, then his toil is in vain and this uselessness reveals itself most clearly at the sight of death. The sentence of Genesis 3, 17-19 expresses then in respect to labor, what Ecclesiastes realizes concerning the uselessness of our work: "And I detested all the fruits of my labor under the sun, because I must leave them to a man who is to come after me. And who knows whether he will be a wise man or a fool? Yet he will have control over all the fruits of my wise labor under the sun. This also is vanity . . ., for what profit comes to a man from all the toil and anxiety of heart with which he has labored?"[59]

Moreover, man's work now stands outside the love which men should have toward one another. Evidence of this is seen in another biblical story in relation to the Fall, namely, that of the Tower of Babel.[60] It is very significant that in this story God does not punish the pride of these men by causing the downfall of their building but by making it impossible for them any longer to understand one another. It is not work, production, civilization that is directly struck by sin. Sometimes it seems that, as man turns farther away from God, he becomes more successful as a builder of the world— although it may be an illusion to see a causal connection between the two, just as it may be an illusion even to interpret certain facts as such a turning away from God.

---

[59]Ecclesiastes 2, 18-23.
[60]"Let us go down and there confuse their language so that they will not understand one another's speech." Gen. 11, 1-9.

In any case, sin does not directly affect labor. After all, work does not constitute the whole of human existence and is not an expression of man's whole life. Hence there is no direct repercussion of man's attitude toward God and fellow-man, whether natural or supernatural, in man's labor. On the other hand, that attitude is truly felt in labor—though it might not be explicit—as a sort of background. That is why sin will be felt also in the world of labor.

When the men of Babel no longer understood one another, they stopped building the Tower,[61] although they could have finished it by making use of foreign slaves or could have used it as a fortress in their wars. Through sin man enters into a world where he can no longer love. It is to such a world that Sartre's philosophy applies, and it is of such a world also that his philosophy is the expression. Slavery, the exploitation of workers, delivering them to inhuman conditions and forms of labor, and, on the other hand, unbridled competition, economic concentration of power, colonialism, economic wars, and labor in the service of war—all these are signs of the dominion which sin exercises in the world of labor.

This statement is not simply literature. By sin man fell from the realm of love—any kind of love—and his work bears the marks of it. St. Thomas, who today is readily quoted as the patron of the optimistic view of fallen man, says that it is impossible for man to love God above all things with a "natural" love, without the help of grace.[62]

It stands to reason that the same man nevertheless possesses the power to love, for he remains man. His whole being in fact tends to love. He desires to receive love and also to give it. But in our actual supernatural order, it is not possible for us to love God with our natural powers if supernatural love is not present. Love is always an orientation of the whole lover. It is a consecration with the whole heart and with all one's powers. This is not possible on the natural level alone, for this natural level exists in fact only as taken up in the concrete orientation toward God.

---

[61]"They stopped building the city." Gen. 11, 8.
[62]*Summa theol.,* p. I-IIae q. 109, a. 3.

To love God is to love Him as we in reality must love Him. That means both supernaturally and naturally. Now the second commandment is like the first. The love of our neighbor is but the reverse side of our love of God. It means loving others in God and loving God in them. That is why a natural love of our neighbor is impossible without supernatural love. Where there is not love of the neighbor, there all relationships between men have lost their fullness and integrity. It is still possible to have relationships of justice among men and to produce and share some values, but even their existence is endangered. Moreover, when sin has done away with supernatural love, human relationships are harmed or at least threatened. This is the sort of repercussion sin has in the world of labor.

We cannot prove experimentally what has been asserted here, for we cannot determine exactly whether others, or we ourselves for that matter, are in the state of sin or in the state of grace. It is likewise impossible to refute our thesis by pointing to the existence of good deeds, good attitudes, a human life animated by love among men who live outside the visible frontiers of Christ's influence, for it is always possible that grace is at work in them in an invisible way.

Not everyone will accept our thesis in its absoluteness, though we believe that it can be concluded legitimately from St. Paul's teaching about the power of sin. If it is not accepted in its universality, it must at least be accepted as applying in most cases, as is done by most theologians. They say that a man who lives outside the influence of grace cannot observe the natural law for a long time. We think that what we have said above about the impossibility of love provides the background for their assertion.

Our thesis is not pessimistic. Nature itself has not suffered any corruption on account of sin, but we no longer possess the power to realize what our nature asks us to realize. Hence our doctrine is not pessimistic about nature as such. Moreover, coupled with it is the optimism of grace.

LABOR AND SALVATION

The influence of sin upon work consists in this that it made man's labor fall from hope and love by the fact and to the extent that mankind abandoned the Covenant with God. The salvation of labor will be accomplished when it can once again be performed in hope and love, by the fact and to the extent that it is executed in a human community for which the covenant of grace has been reestablished. This restoration is accomplished by God in His Son, our Lord Jesus Christ. From the beginning, "all things have been created through and unto Him,"[63] which means that the whole creation is directed to the Covenant with God in Him. God's merciful fidelity upholds, as always, that loving plan in spite of man's infidelity, and He finally sent His Son as our Redeemer.

What did Christ do as our Savior? We say often that he redeemed us by undergoing sufferings and thus reconciled us with God. Let us say rather that Christ brings love even unto His Passion and thus reconciles us with God. The Son brings back the Father's love for us, and He is thus the firstborn of a new humanity which lives once more in love for God and for the fellow-man. No doubt, the Passion is the high point in our Lord's work of salvation—namely, His passion unto death and thereby also unto His Resurrection —but the work of salvation is not confined to the Cross.

The high point of Christ's redeeming work lies in the Cross, because it was there that our total opposition was overcome and that obedience to the Father went to the limit. That high point of the Cross—with the Resurrection as its crowning achievement—summarizes at the same time the whole work of the Lord. However, Christ is also Savior before and after His Cross and Passion. He is that, not merely in name, but in reality. After His Passion, He is Savior as the Glorified One, by making us share fully in His saving love, communicating it to us in His Spirit and through

---

[63] Col. 1, 16.

His Church. He is Savior even before the Passion and Cross, by already offering His love. He offers this love in His public life by His word. This word is not only doctrine or law or an explanatory introduction to His proper work of salvation that is still to follow. On the contrary, it offers and gives, brings and founds the merciful love with which the Father establishes His kingdom among us, makes us children of God and brothers among ourselves.

Even in His hidden life, Jesus is already saving, merely by being among us with that love, by giving us an example of that life, but especially by placing it in our midst in a wordless way. Viewed in this light, His hidden life in Nazareth is a redeeming life for our every-day life and His labor there is a redeeming labor for our labor.

We emphasized a moment ago that labor is not a punishment for sin. Though labor was affected by sin, it is and remains a dominion of man over the earth and consequently a self-development. Let us look at the labor of Jesus in Nazareth from that standpoint. Much lyrical piety has been uttered about Jesus' troubles and poverty, and His despised situation. Together with Mary and Joseph, he is presented as the example of humility and contentment.

It is true that Our Lord did not wish to be wealthy. He labored in the sweat of His brow, He exercised a very simple trade, and practiced humility and obedience in it. But He equally wished to experience in it the joys of living close to nature, of laboring in a way that was still personal. In Nazareth, He learned to be familiar with ordinary daily life. He learned there the peace and security that later would characterize His whole conduct. He also accepted the joy of mastering a small section of earthly reality and He even matured slowly and profoundly in it until His mission called Him elsewhere.

If Nazareth reveals anything about the Incarnate Word, it is how ordinary He was, how faithfully and earnestly He chose "being like unto men,"[64] rather than how humble and

---

[64]Philip. 2, f.

despised He was in that life. If Nazareth teaches us anything, it is the important place work, together with family life,
occupied in His life. So important was labor for the Son of
God that He chose to live and sanctify a working man's life
for so long a time and so profoundly.

Jesus sanctified labor, not by endowing it with technical
perfection, but by performing it out of love, just as He did
not bring us science, art, philosophy, or even principally an
ethics, but the love that should lie at the source and foundation of all these things.

The fact that Jesus performed such a primitive kind of
work in such lowly conditions certainly does not give us
motives for devoutly opposing technology or refusing to fight
for the just rights of the worker. Our Lord's life in Nazareth
teaches us that all those things, inventions, plannings, the
betterment of social conditions, are valuable only if they are
animated by the love He teaches and communicates to us.
Christ's love does not merely inspire our labor, making us
willing to suffer poverty and contempt—although this lesson
is also contained in it—but it also teaches earnest and faithful
professional service of our fellow-man.[65]

Nazareth, then, is not merely a prelude to Calvary in
Christ's salvific activity. It also prefigures His glory. Christ
there suffers the consequences of sin, for sin has affected labor.
But, unlike His Passion, labor is not merely the result of sin
alone. Christ accepts and sanctifies labor as belonging to
man's very existence. That is why Nazareth signifies fidelity
to His incarnation and also foreshadows His glory, the glory
in which He fills our whole life with His Spirit of liberty
and love.

---

[65]It seems to us that this idea suggests a turn in the devotion to
Our Lord's hidden life in Nazareth. It has offered the worker con-
solation in his toil and poverty, but it can also serve to animate
and Christianize labor itself. Cf. Y. de Montcheuil, S. J., "Le mystère
de Nazareth et la rédemption du travail," *Problèmes de la vie
spirituelle,* Paris, 1947, p. 150; also the spiritual writings of Charles
de Foucauld, see René Voillaume, *Seeds of the Desert, the Legacy
of Charles de Foucauld,* Chicago, 1955.

When we look at Nazareth in that light of faith, we see not only the humble Carpenter but also the King who establishes in all things human the "kingdom of truth, love and peace," a kingdom which He will hand over to the Father. We can learn about Christ's kingship in Nazareth, although some might have preferred to honor Him there as "Christ the Worker." In any case, we should not say that the Feast of Christ the King has put Christ in the "ruling class." As long as anyone yields a little to that idea, the title of "Christ the Worker" will have an "unredeemed" meaning, and be unworthy of the Savior. The title of King—as given in the Old Testament and especially in the way Christ declared Himself to be such, namely, in His whole appearance as Messias, by His humble entry into Jerusalem, and His avowal before Pilate—is free from all the earthly, narrow, and sinful connotations that are so often attached to it.

We can likewise purify the title of "worker," removing from it all Marxist, humanistic and also devoutly patronizing meanings that are given to the term. We can then honor the Lord as Worker in an untroubled vision of faith.

We see, then, that Christ's life and sufferings do not oblige us to try to permeate the labor of His disciples exclusively with a *mystique* of the Cross. Our earthly labor, no doubt, will always have its share of burdens and sufferings, and a true cross will be attached to it as long as work is affected by sin, which means as long as we are on earth. However, it is also possible to "redeem" labor and bring it back to its essential nature, which is that of subduing the earth in an atmosphere of fellowship with, and service of, our fellow-men.

No doubt, labor, especially our modern industrial labor with everything that goes with it, will for a long time remain primarily a cross modern man has to bear. At the same time, our Christian hope can make us look forward to an increasing realization of man's dominion over the earth, by the fact that love is re-established more and more because of the growing influence of Christ. An investigation among Catholic workers in France revealed that the consciousness of wretchedness predominates in their milieu of labor. The technologists have a more optimistic view; they see the grandeur of their position of mastery over matter.[66]

This certainly should prompt us not to develop a one-sided *mystique* of labor, which finds expression solely in a lyric "consecration of the world." Nevertheless, we must not forget that Christ's Resurrection can project its light also on the world of labor and that there also we should hope for and encounter the Savior's light and love.

LABOR AND MAN'S FINAL FULFILLMENT

Salvation can more and more permeate labor, and labor itself, together with culture, can make us grow in a sanctified and redeemed human existence. This brings us to the last point we wish to discuss, namely, labor in relation to man's final fulfillment. Only then will a theology of labor not seem to be an illusion when it is understood that the future life will not rob our earthly labors of their meaning and value. Only when labor, seen in the light of eternity, appears to have its value, will it seem to be more than an empty killing of time during our earthly life. We hope to show here that it has such a positive value. Before we can do this, we must first arrive at a correct view of that final fulfillment itself.

Catholic theology and instruction have for a long time dealt with the resurrection of the body, the gathering of the elect, the completion of the world, the initiation of "new heavens and a new earth wherein dwells justice,"[67] in which God will be "all in all,"[68] as if they were given into the bargain after *souls* attain their own blessedness.

This blessedness of *souls,* which was thought of principally as the blessedness of every separate soul, was said to consist primarily in seeing, the eternal seeing of God's Being, by which the soul is enraptured in love. One can say that such an idea of man's heavenly fulfillment is too

---

[66]M. de. Certeau, "La prière des ouvriers," *Christus, Cahiers spirituels,* 1957, pp. 413-427, especially p. 425 and its notes.
[67]2 Pet. 3, 13.
[68]1 Cor. 15, 28.

narrow, due to the fact that it is described from the stand-point of mystical ecstasy, of contemplation.

Gustave Thils prefers to see the final fulfillment from the standpoint of Christ's life on earth, in which He both saw the Father and at the same time *labored* on earth: "In that case, blessedness would be at the same time very heavenly and very earthly."[69] In fact, we should not think of eternal bliss solely as of a mystical ecstasy. It should rather be compared to the complete *mystique,* which precisely transcends ecstasy or the absorption of the faculties, and peacefully unfolds in an activity that sometimes is relentless. We should really compare it above all to both Jesus' contemplation and His activity, to His life in the intimacy with the Father and His mission on earth.

Nevertheless, it seems to us that this blessedness must not be compared solely to labor, or even to a combination of contemplation and activity. We believe that it can also be looked upon as pure contemplation, understood not as a solitary individual function and a merely interior vision, but as a contemplative communion with others, which is, as we have seen, the opposite pole of labor in our earthly life. For, doesn't Scripture tell us that heaven is a festive banquet? Perhaps it is even better to say that the whole distinction between work and contemplation is something that belongs to earth and that therefore beatitude transcends as well as includes both. Then, however, we must also add that the unfulfilled part of the work, by which man continues to conquer the earth and realize himself, the struggle with nature and the battle against evil, will no longer exist.

Although Christ's life on earth comes close to what our blessedness will be, the fundamental prototype of that blessedness is His *glorified* life. Here He no longer works in an earthly sense. He no longer struggles or battles. He rules. And we can rule with Him. We shall sit on thrones with Him, not in passive solemnity, but with the joyful mobility

---

[69]G. Thils, "Espérance et sense chrétien de l'histoire," *Lumen Vitae,* Vol. 9, 1954, pp. 493-504. The quotation is found on p. 497.

of guests at a banquet table. We readily admit that in Heaven man will forever penetrate more profoundly into God's mystery, but all struggle and strife will be over.

Having looked at the final fulfillment from the standpoint of our entire existence, which includes labor, we can now ask ourselves what relation labor has to that final fulfillment. As long as we pay attention solely to the individual blessedness of our souls, it is impossible to show any other relation of that beatitude to labor than the fact that the good intentions of our work will be rewarded with a heavenly recompense. But, if we look at the future world as a completion of mankind and of the whole of creation, and, on the other hand, see labor as a humanization of the world and also of ourselves, then both lie somewhat in each other's perspective and the question regarding their relations is a pressing one. The problem has in fact become such in modern theology.

That is why the problem concerning the relation between what we now build upon earth and the final fulfillment constantly appears in the immense literature concerning labor, civilization, culture, history, and Christian humanism. It is not at all a question of the relation of labor, considered from the purely natural standpoint, with the completed creation. What we ask is: Is labor, as sanctified and redeemed in Christ, a positive preparation for the new earth in which God's justice dwells? If so, to what extent do our labor and our whole activity by which we make history contribute to it?

At first sight, we discern a line, an ascent, but there will nevertheless also be a leap between this world—which is "passing away,"[70] so much so that it is pictured as passing away "with great violence"[71]—and the new one.

In all probability, there is both continuity and discontinuity between the two. That is why either one or the other of these two aspects is strongly emphasized in modern theological thought. In fact the two tendencies have been designated by special names. The proponents of one are called "incarnationists" and the others "eschatologists." Between these two

[70] 1 Cor. 7, 31.
[71] 2 Pet. 3, 10; Apoc. 21, 1.

there are several intermediary positions.[72] Let us here mention a few points that may be important for the development of a synthetic view in this matter.

There is, first of all, continuity between a redeemed labor and the future world. The latter is truly constructed to some extent by ourselves. For it is this, our world, that will be renewed, just as (i.e., because, and to the extent that) this, our body, will rise again. It is by virtue of one and the same Savior that a new world is already being built now and that the world will be fully new then. The same love that Christ brought us rules and animates both. With the incarnation of God's Son—whence the term "incarnationism"—the newness has already begun. It will be completed when He finally returns. These are the principal aspects of continuity.

But there is also discontinuity. There is a gap, and consequently a leap, between this world and the world of the future —and even between everything that is already redeemed and is realized in virtue of salvation on the one hand, and the final fulfillment on the other. The difference is not only quantitative, but also qualitative, just as (i.e., because, and to the extent that) our body will then be completed and be incorruptible.[73]

On earth, nothing attains completion; everything is partial only. One form of civilization and culture is followed by another. This succession is almost always achieved by partly breaking down what went before. This destruction is necessary, because what we realize and fulfill in this world is not only an expression of ourselves but also a limitation. This limitation and incompleteness that is proper to our earthly time must disappear. But even more must disappear the

[72]For fairly popular description of both tendencies see Gustave Thils *Transcendance ou Incarnation*, 1953, or also P. Smulders "De zin der geschiedenis," *Streven*, vol. 8, No. I (1955), pp. 385-395. A more detailed description with extensive bibliography is given by L. Malevez, "Deux théologies catholiques de l'histoire," *Bijdragen*, vol. 10, 1949, pp. 225-240.

[73]"So also with the resurrection of the dead. What is sown in corruption rises in incorruption; what is sown in dishonor rises in glory; what is sown in weakness rises in power; what is sown a natural body rises a spiritual body." 1 Cor. 15, 42-44.

power of sin, which has not yet been taken away by the glorification of Christ.

The ruler of this world has been overcome, but he still has power, and he makes his influence felt in all human creations. Nothing as yet is completely taken up in love. It is precisely this aspect of discontinuity that is so powerfully described in the scriptural accounts of the catastrophes that will accompany Christ's second coming.

However, something that is purely positive lies hidden behind the declarations regarding the passing character of earthly things. What we have just now summed up as characteristics that must disappear is itself negative: the loss of achievements, disregard, the limitations proper to the incompleted, the destruction wrought by evil. Precisely this limitation itself disappears with the entry of the final fulfillment, when decay itself will decay.

This we can hear in the words of Scripture, where it is said that Christ then will destroy death as the last enemy.[74] This means that what is positive will remain, what is positive everywhere and always, which everyone bears with him in his person, even if he was not able to give expression to it or if that expression was misunderstood or destroyed. When we see that what was annihilation and loss is itself annihilated, the words of Scripture concerning "harvesting" and "gathering" get their full meaning. The jolt of transition is then a leap to a full flowering.

Is it possible to draw a single picture in which both the continuity and discontinuity between this life and the final fulfillment are emphasized? Let us cast a look upon our earthly life as a whole. Life, even that of plants, proceeds by leaps. How much more this is true of our own human life, particularly for civilized man! Between the periods of our life there is, every time, a crisis, a birth.[75] Much of what was built in a previous period is torn down, everything falls apart, but the deepest core of it emerges again with greater maturity.

---

[74] 1 Cor. 15, 26.
[75] Cf. Romano Guardini, *Die Lebensalter,* 1959, Würzburg, 1959. R. Troisfontaines, *Je ne meurs pas,* 1961.

It is not only natural life which has such a continuity within discontinuity. Even more our life of grace, has these two elements, and they usually go together in it. We can also point to something similar in our social life. It exists on a small scale, for example, in the relationship between parents and their children, or between husband and wife, but it is also found, on a larger scale, in the life of a specific civilization.

There is similar continuity and discontinuity between this life and the future life in Christ. The discontinuity is realized for everyone in death, but for the whole of humanity in the second coming of Our Lord. And this last leap is greater than any death or birth within our earthly existence, for it is the end of all birth and death. In these there is also continuity, for nothing is lost but everything is harvested.

"Unless the grain of wheat falls into the ground and dies, it remains alone. But if it dies, it brings forth much fruit."[76] Jesus Himself applies the law of growth and fulfillment through death to us. He spoke those words shortly before His own glorification through His Passion, and hence they are applicable first of all to Himself and then to us. The growth of the grain of wheat is only a foreshadowing of what can be accomplished in the life of the man blessed with grace, but Christ's own fulfillment is the prototype of this growth. We have to undergo death through persecution and by suffering the contempt and disregard of men, but also by making the sacrifice of earthly values, because we are in Him, and to the extent that we are in Him. At the same time, our union with Him already now makes us heavenly men, and so the law of preservation and continuity is founded on Him, together with the law of the loss of one's life.

We have gone to great lengths to show that labor has an important place and role, not only in our human life, but also in our life for God in Christ. Labor, then, is not a pastime but a fulfillment of life. It is even the building of our life in relation to the final fulfillment. We cooperate in the construction of the final community of love by the work we are doing now. And then we shall behold what we are now in the process of building.

[76]John 12, 24.

CHAPTER SIX

A NEW HEAVEN AND A NEW EARTH[1]

This chapter is not a study of Biblical theology strictly speaking, although we use principally Biblical data. Without any doubt dogmatic theology must not be confused with Biblical theology, since in the first place, besides Scripture, dogmatic theology has Tradition and the Magisterium of the Church as its formal basis. Nevertheless, these two sources have added little to Biblical data concerning eschatology. Even the images used in modern eschatology are mostly borrowed from Scripture. In the Middles Ages, only two points were defined: 1. The beatific vision or eternal damnation can be attained before the last judgment; 2. The existence of a purification, called "Purgatory."[2] The new-born Church had an awareness of the first point. Later declarations only assert that communion with Christ between death and His second coming, attains substantially the same beatitude as that which will follow His Parousia. Therefore, since the Bible, the matter of eschatology has remained practically the same.

The perspective, however, has altered. The statements we have just mentioned chiefly fix attention on the fate of *"souls"* during the interval preceding the Parousia. The Magisterium's judgments inevitably leave much in the shade. But it can be regretted that theology, preaching and devotion have focussed one-sidedly on the content of these judgments: the fate of the faithful after death. For instance, before 1948, the Dutch Catechism contained this question: "Is there another judgment besides the particular one?" The Baltimore Catechism still asks: "If every one is judged immediately after death, why will there be a general judgment?"

---

[1] Reprinted, with slight changes, from *Lumen Vitae*, September, 1963.
[2] Cf. Denziger, nos. 456, 464, 530 ff., 694, 983.

We can rejoice over the notable change in present day theology and preaching toward the Biblical perspective: a Christian aspect of the future life is being revived. This chapter heartily welcomes this return. With Holy Scripture, we will speak of eternal life not as offered to *souls* in heaven, but to *men* in a new creation. That is why we have given this dogmatic exposition a Biblical title: "A new heaven and a new earth."[3]

Therefore, we will treat the same subject as Holy Scripture does, but we will try to arrange and develop the data of revelation both in their mutual connection and in comparison with our human knowledge,[4] and especially with our modern existential experience and outlook on the future. We will try to describe eternal life, starting from our present human life, as Scripture does. In this way we hope not to forget that eschatological revelation is essentially sober, not ordained for knowledge but for hope. For these reasons, we will begin this chapter with a few observations on the interpretation of eschatological data, chiefly borrowed from Karl Rahner.[5] They are of a nature to make us see better not only what is tributary to the epoch in the Biblical expression, but principally, what is immutable as divine promise.

Because of its re-orientation toward the "last end," still more because of its "demythizing" interpretation, at present eschatology is a question for study rather than popular publications. In eschatology, "the theological workshop is provisionally closed for alterations," to quote Hans Urs von Balthasar, who has sketched a very instructive survey of this workshop.[6] For the same reason, what follows, matter and method, is put forward for discussion, wherever of course, there is no question of articles of faith already defined. A chatechist could only justifiably make use of it, insofar as he himself recognizes revelation in it and, above all—this

---

[3] Is. 65, 17; 2 Pet. 3, 13; Apoc. 21, 1.
[4] Cf. Denziger, no. 1796.
[5] "Theologische Prinzipien der Hermeneutik eschatologischer Aussagen," *Schriften zur Theologie*, vol. IV, Einsiedeln, 1960, pp. 401-428.
[6] "Eschatologie," *Fragen der Theologie Heute,* p. 404.

is extremely important—insofar as he is able to make his hearers see revelation in it. Under these conditions we trust that the matter found here will be useful.

INTERPRETATION OF ESCHATOLOGICAL DATA

The Place of Eschatology. What Scripture tells us of eternal life is not a communication, but a promise. It is neither information about the time coming, a story about the future, nor an impersonal prognosis, but a promise made by one person to another. To develop this better, we will say something about divine language, and even language in general.

Human language speaks about *something.* At the same time, it is the language *of* someone, someone who discloses himself, reveals himself in talking about something. Finally it is talking *to* someone, to whom not only the speaker says something, but reveals himself and enters in a communion with him. Each of these three moments can prevail and predominate in the conversation, while the two others only serve the predominant moment. Thus, we can first speak of something, give information, announce some news. Then there is the expression of one's inner self, the personal testimony. Lastly, there is the language that creates union: a whole scale lies there, from a casual greeting to a declaration of love. In this last kind of language everything aims at the communion of persons. The person speaking expresses himself precisely, as being for, of and with, the other.

We think that God's language in His revelation is of this kind. He offers us salvation, purifying and enriching communion with Himself. In a word, God offers Himself. God's word does not contain objective information, liable to another meaning outside this communication of Himself. This applies to the world—intraworldly relations are subjects of our human research—and to God, intra-Trinity relations being revealed that we may share in them. Even personal testimony in revelation is only valuable insofar as it expresses what God is to us, and what we are to Him. All revealed truths come back to this existential relation. Obviously, only the Magisterium of the Church can judge this thesis in the last resort, and the conclusions we draw from it. But we think it can be put forward without temerity, because we do not see that it opposes any dogma; on the contrary, in this way each dogma is rightly situated in the economy of redemption. For what concerns eschatology, this can be judged from what follows.

Our human existence is always in the present; it belongs to the present, but at the same time it is settled in it by our past, and orientated toward the future. That is why God tells us who He is for us, and who we are for Him, both as regards our past, even in its remotest origin, and our future, even our definitive and everlasting future. In other words, God's Revelation has an eschatological and a protological aspect. Protology and eschatology, therefore, have the same character which we have just attributed to revelation as a whole. The eschatological revelation of God, then, is the promise of eternal salvific communion, while protology tells us what were the original relations between God and man. They are not a "report" either on the past or the future; they are not meant to complete human knowledge in paleontology or historical prognosis; they speak to our faith which, especially concerning echatological revelation, "is in God as our hope."[7] We will make this clearer by speaking of the content and form of eschatology.

Content of Eschatology. The content of eschatology is already outlined in what we have written above: it is revelation of God, insofar as it is a promise concerning our future. That implies two things: 1. Eschatology is the revelation itself of God under a fixed aspect; 2. It regards a real future.

Eschatology is an aspect of revelation as a whole; it is not a separate chapter, still less an appendix. If this revela-

---

[7] 1 Pet. 1, 21.

tion was a series of concrete information, eschatology could be what it often has been for our theology and catechesis: "a harmless little final chapter" (Karl Barth). In reality it is what it becomes more and more in theology and catechesis: the aspect of promise of the "communing" language of God. Everything is said by the very fact that God contracts alliance with men and is faithful to it. It is not speculative considerations on a starry world or a sojourn of souls that leads Israel to eschatology, it is simply their faith in this faithful God. In the measure that the lives of men on earth are enlightened by divine contact, that eschatology becomes more complete. The most fundamental fact of God's alliance with his people gives them the intuition that a day will come, the Day of the Lord, when they will become a great people; then will the images of the earthly paradise and the promised land become a full reality. The prophets insist that alliance with God will be ineffectual without the people's fidelity and justice; that is why, from Amos onward, the Day of the Lord is a day of judgment, whereas from Isaias, the Messianic blessedness is the lot of the faithful Remainder. After the Captivity, personal responsibility becomes more and more prominent.[8] Thus it is gradually admitted that ultimately judgment and salvation will come to each one individually, even those already in the sleep of death. Even then, we must wait for the martyrdom of the heroes of faith at the epoch of the Macchabees before the resurrection is unambiguously professed, and with it the eternal life which transcends history. In the New Testament, eschatology is also the consequence of our present state in relation to the redemption. Here everything flows from the universal significance of Christ's redemption; the novelty of the New Testament eschatology consists in the fact that the Day of Yahweh turns into the day of Christ, while future happiness with God becomes unending communion with Our Lord in the Father's House. Union with Our Lord sheds

---

[8]Ez. 18.

its light on the fate of those who are asleep in Him before His return. Finally, within the development of Church tradition, the dogma of Mary's assumption can be considered as a consequence of the gradual discovery of her place in the economy of the redemption.

If eschatology is the aspect of promise of all revelation, that does not mean that it is always perceived as the conclusion of man's actual relation to God's salvation. The inverse can arise. The beginnings of God's dealings with men can be compared to the love of betrothed, which expresses itself in a promise of life-long fidelity. It was chiefly in the light of promise that Abraham walked in God's presence. It was the same for the Israelites in the desert, with this difference, that the Israelites already enjoyed the essence of the blessings of the Promised Land, that is, the presence of Yahweh Himself.

So there is an intimate bond between the promise and our present situation as regards the redemption. Yet this promise concerns a real future. We have to be on our guard against an interpretation that leaves nothing to the prophecies but an appeal for faith and fidelity in the present. In the same sense Karl Rahner accepts an *Entapokalyptisierung,* of which we shall speak later, but will not hear of an *Enteschatologisierung.*[8a] God does not try to humor us, He takes us seriously. He takes us as He created us, as beings in process of self-development. That is why He promises us His salvation, even as our future. Since He is God, He promises salvation for our definitive and ultimate future for always, for our eternity.

This future, however, and the path leading to it are integrated in relations which are personal on both sides, and which constitute our actual salvation. This future differs radically from a future at a concrete level, foreseen by physical, biological and economic laws, over which we have power by calculation, even if our computations are incom-

---

[8a]"Entapokalyptisierung" is the removal of apocalyptic features; "Enteschatologisierung" is the removal of eschatological features. Ed.

plete. The future of a personal relation is unpredictable in its concrete form; it can be guaranteed by love and fidelity, but the latter remain exposed to the imperfections of human liberty. Our future salvation is assured by God, but God's ways are not ours. The name God gave Himself, "I am who am," expresses simultaneously a faithful presence and a sovereign incalculability in its realization. The possibilty of our infidelity, even definitive, makes the future even more unpredictable. What the Old Testament expressed in various ways about God's plans is concentrated by Christ on the moment of His return. It is not for us to know the times and moments which God's authority alone has fixed;[9] it does not even belong to the Son in His earthly existence.[10] This does not only apply to the date, but to everything of a nature to guarantee our definitive future for us. The "result" of God's judgment is unknown to us. We do not know who the damned are, we do not know whether there are any, nor can we be sure there are none. In theological reflection on the eternal fate of the unbaptized, even infants, it is out of place to assert that all are lost, or all saved. Here we are faced with God's own secret, and the adventure of surrender to His love.

Form of Eschatology. When two human beings exchange the promise to unite their lives, they do not do so without forming concrete ideas of this future happiness: home, a way of life, children, happiness. Often these concrete hopes are not realized or vanish, but the normal development of their love will turn their common life into their greatest happiness. Each of us struggles among many illusions, disillusions, "projects" and "counter-projects," more or less conscious. Among all these vicissitudes our fidelity must remain unaltered and grow stronger. Each one will find the same rhythm in his relations with God; when the moment comes for the reality, from a youthful dream, God becomes our greatest support. It is not astonishing that something like this is found in the history of prophecy in Israel.

---

[9] Acts 1, 7.
[10] Mark 12, 32; Mt. 24, 36.

191

According to St. Thomas,[11] it is the infused light which is essential in prophetical grace, not the infused image. The light gives knowledge. The "Seers" of Israel did not receive principally celestial visions or dictates, but a faithful insight into historical reality. When their words concern the future— for their admonitions touch both past and present—they express the promise of God's merciful fidelity, and therefore, of the final redemption, under the form of what seems to them to be its supreme realization for the people, for humanity, for each individual. This explains why the Day of Yahweh for them means the restoration of Israel and of the house of David, of peace between men and even animals. For the same reason, the final and transcendent kingdom of the New Testament appears in the Apocalypse under similar images. Not only the end of all things is described in this way, unchanging images depict its approach: Yahweh and Christ appear in a tremendous upheaval of the entire universe, even in what seemed to the Jews to be the most stable: the sun, moon and stars. All that expresses the dawn of new relations between God and men. Other details are secondary. This shows in the divergence among the writers: the "place" for man's definitive condition is a city or a banquet-hall; the end comes when some men are still living, or after the earth has been destroyed by fire, etc.

All this applies particularly to prophecies of apocalyptic form. The apocalypse is a literary style of Jewish origin, dating between 200-100 B.C., during the Macchabean persecution. Today we would refer to it as religious underground resistance literature. It centers on this topic: for the moment the powers hostile to God triumph; but a new era will dawn when the tables will be turned. The end of history, the last judgment and final situation are beheld by the seer in striking and mysterious visions, with symbolic numbers, explanations given by an angel, etc. Under this strange form, authentic faith is coupled with vigorous nationalism. Among apocryphal apocalypses, not forming part of Scripture, some are

---

[11]*Summa theol.*, p. II-II, q. 173, a. 2.

very religious, such as Esdras IV and the book of Henoch. In Scripture itself there are passages or entire books which are apocalyptic, e.g., Ezechiel, 40-48; Isaia, 24-27; Zach., 9-14; Joel 3 ff.; Daniel; Mark, 13; and particularly St. John's Apocalypse. Comparing non-canonical and inspired apocalypses, we notice that in the latter the visionary element is much more restrained. We find there for certain the guarantee of a prophetic vision in faith. This does not answer the question whether these visions proceed from an ecstatic state or whether they are based on a literary fiction. It must be emphatically stressed that the apocalyptic genre is a way of preaching hope and the promise, not a report of the future. We are not considering whether it is possible, abstractly speaking, for God in his omniscience—taken eventually as conceptual knowledge—to give man an anticipated knowledge of the future, independent of his present existential experience, as a kind of "second sight." It seems to us that in real prophecy, even apocalyptic, the divine promise starts from present existential experience: such as I am with you now I shall remain, Conqueror, Judge and faithful to my promise.

All this shows once more that eschatological revelations do not aim to present computations of time and even less definitions of place or physical structure. The phenomena which will mark the end of our present world are not matter for revelation, any more than the place "where heaven is." Heaven, moreover, is a state, and the relation of the glorified bodies of Our Lord and Our Lady to our earth, cannot be thought of as a material distance, expressed in miles or in light years. Our bodies and our earth will be in an unimaginably glorified state. There is no biology of glorified humanity, at the most is there an extremely reserved anthropology. So we must not interpret apocalyptic descriptions materially, but neither may we spiritualize them to the extent of a disincarnation; we should rather personalize them. The basic categories of eschatological revelation are personal ones: the lordship of God over us, our communion with Christ, a dwelling together in a paradise or city, celebrating divine praise at the marriage-feast of the Lamb. Finally, it concerns God as He gives Himself to us. Hans Urs von Balthasar has very aptly said: "God is the final end of His creature. He is Heaven if we deserve Him, Hell if we lose Him, Judgment when He tries us, Purgatory when He makes us expiate."[12]

A NEW HEAVEN AND A NEW EARTH

Having spoken of hermeneutic principles, we must now see what revelation says of eternal life itself. Following what the prophets, Christ and the apostles teach us, we must see the perfection of eternal life as prolongation of our human existence and of the redemption already accomplished. This life is perfect; so we must eliminate from our theological notions all that is imperfect. When we speak of God we use negative-positive conceptions; we have to do the same here, and our last word is that no eye has seen what God prepares for those He loves. Nevertheless, with moderation, we must speak to justify and express our faith which is also our hope.

God Gives Himself to Us. Our theology of heaven is very interested in the activity of man in the immediate contemplation of God. But, as in every treatise, we must first speak of what God does. It will not be enough to use too abstract terms such as "God" or the "Divine Essence." God has given himself concretely in the history of salvation; He will do the same in its completion. The Father will give himself through the Son in the Holy Spirit. This means that the three Persons will not be merely contemplated as from without; the Holy Spirit will fill us more than ever, and thus unite us to the Son, so that only then shall we be in plenitude the children of the Father. The whole economy of the Christian redemption will remain, but manifest and accomplished. Therefore will the Son remain Man and one of us. If it is written that Christ will give back the kingdom to God the Father and

---

[12]*Op. cit.,* p. 407.

that the Son will be subject to him,[13] it in no way means that the Son will cease to be man. The contrary is suggested when the Apocalypse says that the Lamb will reign for ever with God,[14] and St. Paul says he hopes to be with the Lord for ever.[15] The mediation of Christ will be over in the sense that neither He, nor any minister of His Church, will take God's place for us, nor ours before Him. For this reason, Christ's royalty will no longer be distinguished from the Father's, nor will He intercede in our favor, since "the Father Himself loves us."[16] Thanks to the Incarnation of the Word, we have immediate contact with God even now, because He is the Father, and the Father in Him. But on earth this contact is veiled by the mediation of ministers, which will cease at the Parousia. "Through Christ" will give way to "with Christ" and "in Christ," and these last two relations will not cease to derive from the Incarnation. If Christ is no longer the mediator, he remains the living Center. The Father, then, will manifest Himself to us for all eternity in the human countenance of Christ, while on our side, we will share the love and contemplation of Christ Himself.

That also means that in eternity God remains author of His works and of His gifts. It is not we who have reached and who possess Him; He will be acting and giving, as when we were on earth. Humanly speaking, He will do so more than ever. We will remain in a receptive attitude, not assuming one of conquest. We shall not "understand" the Blessed Trinity as if we had solved a problem. Even in the contemplation of heaven, God will remain "incomprehensible," unattainable, impenetrable for us. His mystery will envelop us, and be the source of our adoration and joy. The shadows of faith will fall away, but our surrender to Him will remain.

God will give Himself *to us,* to each and to all. The human community will not break up in eternal life. In the Father's House and in Christ Glorified men will be more

---

[13] 1 Cor. 15, 24-30.
[14] Apoc. 21, 22; 22, 1-3.
[15] 1 Thess. 4, 17.
[16] John 16, 27.

closely united. God always wants unity among men, but in eternity this union will be consummated. We will no longer be strangers to one another, and every relation that is different from love will disappear. God will be all in everyone, and on that account, all of us will be fully ourselves, individually and for others.

To Contemplate and to Love. God will give Himself to us. That means, we will be in communion with God and with all the elect. "Communion" says everything, but we will grasp its worth better if we analyze its component parts: contemplation and love.

We will contemplate God, directly, without the intermediacy of creatures or the shadows of faith. We shall no longer reason over God's being from His works, we shall see His very self. No longer effects, but His essence, will determine our knowledge. Obviously, there is question here of a spiritual activity, but the word "see" is the best, since sight affords the clearest and fullest knowledge. Sight engenders insight. But God does not exhibit Himself as a thing; God shows Himself as a person. We find this in the Bible, when there is question of seeing the face of God. The face shows us not only a person's natural self, but also his intimate personality which he reveals in looking at us.

We shall not look at God, we shall regard Him, and He will regard us. We will not only see His countenance, but there will be "face to face" contact. When St. Paul uses this expression,[17] speaking of the end of time, he borrows it from the Old Testament: "God spoke to Moses face to face, as a man speaks to his friend."[18] What was then accorded to one man for a moment, will be the lot of all for ever. For Moses and the prophets, theophanies always entailed a mission and a message. The vision on Thabor concluded with these words to the apostles: "Hear him." It is rather doubtful that this vision of God really surpassed the mediacy of earthly contact. This explains the later phrase that Moses saw God "from

---

[17] 1 Cor. 13, 12.
[18] Ex. 33, 11; Deut. 34, 10.

behind."[19]   St. John asserts: "No one has seen God at any time."[20] So what is given to the elect in heaven is quite different: message yields to contemplation, audition to vision.

It is good to remember that the expression "face to face" has its origin in the description of a conversation. It is in conversation that revelation of ourselves is a gift of the highest degree, for words are the clearest revelation of self, especially in an intimate conversation. Nevertheless, words are not enough to reveal the integral reality; no one can express himself fully in words. That is why "face to face" is the best image of our external contact with God. This contact can be compared to a deeper intuitive contact; the image of the heavenly Jerusalem compared to a bride is suggestive in this sense, but in the end, all images are powerless to express the intimacy and plenitude of the gift God will make of Himself.

We have spoken already of communication with God in knowledge which involves love. Even more than their knowledge, the love of the elect can be called "beatifying," since "it is a more blessed thing to give than to receive."[21] If knowledge eliminates the darkness and errors which proceed from mediation, love will exclude all struggle against sin, and whatever could cause deviation on account of earthly cares and labors. If knowledge which is vision is no longer a "having" but a "being with," then love is *a fortiori* possession by being possessed. Love is a continual absorption in God, a rest that, at the same time, is an unrest because we are possessed by God: "They are before the throne of God, serving Him night and day in His temple."[22] On one side, we can say that perfect love is rest. On the other, "resting from their labors,"[23] also means that the love which incites the elect will only be fully active in eternity. Nothing shows us better this activity of love, than the doxologies and thanksgivings that abound in the Apocalypse. Thus will the wor-

[19] Ex. 33, 23.
[20] John 1, 18.
[21] Acts 20. 35.
[22] Apoc. 7, 15.
[23] Apoc. 14, 13.

ship on earth attain its perfection in heaven. The rites of oblation, the sacrifice of Christ and His servants will become an attitude of oblation; only in this way can we speak of a "celestial sacrifice."

Love for our neighbor is assimilated to the love for God even on earth, but even more so at the end of time. Even now the knowledge of God cannot be dissociated from the knowledge of creatures. The communion with God will be the most intimate possible for each one; it will have a name which none but the bearer knows. At the same time, there will be perfect communion among the elect, just because God will be all *in all.* It will be the perfect community of the Trinity, assuming all the elect within itself. "Behold the tabernacle of God with men; and He will dwell with them. And they shall be His people, and God Himself with them shall be their God."[24]

The Body and the World. Man will not only have his body and soul in the life to come; in a certain way, his world will be there too. Jewish thought found it quite normal that the resurrection should include the whole man. Faced with the Greek inclination to dualism, it was necessary to declare emphatically that this resurrection concerned the body too. Since St. Paul,[25] the Church has often done this.[26] The affirmation of man's resurrection with a real human body is formal.[27] This human body will be his: "We believe . . . in the resurrection of this body which we now carry and not any other";[28] "they will rise with their own bodies."[29] These declarations must be understood as denying man's dualist disincarnation or a de-humanization (a pure spiritualization, volatilization) of his body. They affirm the identification of the risen body and the earthly body, precisely within the identity of the person; they underline the fact

---

[24] Apoc. 21, 3.
[25] 1 Cor. 15, 35-38.
[26] Denzinger, nos. 40, 427, 429, 464, 531.
[27] Denzinger, no. 207.
[28] Denzinger, no. 427.
[29] Denzinger, no. 429.

that God's promise concerns each one of us in our full existence. They are not answers to certain physical or biological
questions, e.g., whether each man will rise again "from his
mortal remains"; whether the vegetative functions will be
active in the next life, etc.

We have already said it, a biology of our future life is impossible; at the most can a very restrained anthropology be
outlined. Starting from the earthly growth of the human
person in his body, we can in some way describe, negatively
and positively, his final state. St. Paul [30] gives a series of
contrasts between the earthly and the glorified body: mortal-
immortal; corruptible-incorruptible; humbled-glorified; pow-
erless-powerful; psychic-spiritual. These contrasts allude first
to the respective states of imperfect and of perfect redemption and secondly to human development and accomplishment.
We think this last contrast can be expressed thus: during
his earthly existence, the human person always somehow
faces his body as pre-given; in heaven, his life will spring
entirely from within, and his body will be fully his. That is
why growth will no longer be necessary, nor the deepening
of perfect possession of oneself. We will also cease to be,
in our bodies, a source of trouble, care or of generation for
others. Birth and procreation will be excluded; our brethren will be "filled up"[31] in number. The whole physical
being will be personalized. The body will no longer be a
mask, a veil, or an obstacle to the revelation of ourselves,
it will be a means of expression, as our face is now (with
the difference that it will not be so "involuntarily." Openness of our being toward others and to the world will be
complete. The body will no longer be an object of abstraction but of intuition. The passing intuition of beauty or love
is a distant sign of this.

On earth, not only the personality can be in opposition
to the body; the personal attitude can oppose the institutional
order. That happens even in the Church, wherein the sacred

---

[30] 1 Cor. 15, 42-44 and 53.
[31] Apoc. 6, 11.

ministry does not necessarily confer holiness, nor is the sacrament dependent upon its minister's holiness. This contrast too will disappear. In the next life there will be no hierarchy or solidarity other than love. Therefore, it seems to us that like marriage the sacerdotal ministry will disappear, but love, brought to maturity in these states, will create "immortal bonds."

What has been said of the body applies also to the world. *Our* world will be glorified too. It will be the same world, but in a perfect state. We do not know what will continue to exist, outside of man, or even whether the world will be reduced or not to transformed humanity. These are questions which remain unanswered. Following what we have said, we can suppose that the world, in so far as it subsists, will be our world in the most perfect manner, in the same way as our bodies will be ours. During our earthly life, we make part of this world our own, not only making it useful, but also to express human feelings, man makes himself a home. In this way, the glorified world will be perfectly ours as well as God's who will live and reign in us; it will be the abode of the Father and of His own. Thus the mission to subdue and rule the earth[32] will be sovereignly accomplished.

We have already stressed that contact with our fellow-men will not disappear in heaven; on the contrary, it will attain perfection. After what has been said about our bodies, we must add that this contact in the future life should not be conceived as taking place in a special zone of activity, beside and apart from, the zone of contact with God Himself. The tendency is to consider immediate knowledge of God as a totally different activity from the knowledge of creatures. In the first knowledge, no creature is an intermediary of knowing,[33] but in the knowledge of creatures, these can become intermediaries pointing to God. The contrast between the two types of knowledge applies only to the vision of God and our

---

[32]Gen. 1, 28.
[33]Cf. Denzinger, no. 530: "Nulla creatura in ratione objecti mediante."

earthly knowledge of creatures, and not to the vision of God and our *celestial* knowledge of the creature. Since as we have said, the body will not be an object of abstractions but of intuition, God will no longer be known through reflection and conclusion starting from creatures, but He will be contemplated in them. The knowledge of creatures could then be simultaneously the knowledge of God in them, just as it could be a knowledge of God acting for, with and in His creatures, and giving Himself to them. If we have inserted this theoretical remark about knowledge, it is not with the intention of abandoning the simplicity of Scriptural language, but on the contrary, to show its value. Anyone who tries to oppose the knowledge of God to the knowledge of creatures in the life to come, will have to separate the words of Scripture into texts which refer to the immediate knowledge of God and texts which refer to relations with our neighbor. Such a division does violence to the texts, which even gainsay it. These texts never contrast the two kinds of knowledge, and nearly all affirm in some way that "God will be all in all." Besides, in heaven we will be "one with Christ," and that evidently refers to His divinity and humanity.

Because we do not experience here below this immediacy of God in His creatures, some of them become a formal sign of God; others veil the relation that exists between God and them behind the intraworldly relations. Thus there is a religious or sacral sphere, next to an humanitarian or profane sphere. This is in no way based upon a binary division in created reality, but upon a polarity in our giving of meaning. The distinction lies in our perception, which discovers a sign of God's presence in some fixed things and activities, while in others it has not this formal experience. This same distinction affects acts, functions, institutions, symbols, but not the being of man and of the world as such. It does not proceed in in the first instance from God but from man, although the Incarnate Word assumed it in His economy of redemption. This distinction will always exist on earth; the Holy Eucharist is not an ordinary meal, and prayer is something different from conversation between friends. And yet, a vivid faith will realize more and more the relativity of the contrast, and *could* express itself in the reduction of religious activities and institutions in favor of what is more implicit: "To find God in all things," which is one of Christianism's tasks. At the end of time all contrast will cease. That is why, on the one hand, everything will be sacred in the new, and especially the heavenly, Jerusalem: "In that day that which is upon the bridle of the horse shall be holy to the Lord; and the caldrons in the house of the Lord shall be as the phials before the altar. And every caldron in Jerusalem and Juda shall be sanctified to the Lord of hosts."[34] But on the other hand, all that is sacred will cease to be made concrete in acts, places and distinct times, for God will be all in all and everything: "I saw no temple therein. For the Lord God almighty is the temple thereof, and the Lamb."[35]

Active Repose. The Jews had their weekly day of rest, the Sabbath. They attributed the observance of this rest to God.[36] Scripture presents the entrance into the promised land[37] or into the future rest[38]; as a participation in this divine Sabbath. The image of heaven as the eternal rest, so rare in Scripture, has found more frequent echo in churchly usage, notably in the liturgical use of IV Esdras, II, 34: "Lord, grant them eternal rest." The Greeks also had their "free time," notably that of "contemplation" which was the privilege of the free man contrasting with "servile work." More or less consciously, scholastic theology characterized celestial happiness in the image of Greek contemplation. Modern feeling differs from this conception, and conceives the future life as social and active. As regards the social aspect of this life we have seen that Scripture bears it out; can the same be said as regards activity?

---

[34]Zach. 14, 20-21.
[35]Apoc. 21, 22.
[36]Gen. 2, 2 ff.
[37]Ps. 95, 11.
[38]Heb. 3, 4-7, 11; cf. Apoc. 14, 13.

We must first examine the starting points of this idea. When the Jews forbade Jesus to heal on the Sabbath, He answered: "My Father works always."[39] The divine Sabbath is active, but so is man's. The Old Testament type of Sabbath is not the torturing idleness of later Judaism, which might be compared with the puritanical Sundays of the nineteenth century; it is the joyous celebration before Yahweh of the Sabbaths anterior to the Captivity.[40] The Sabbath is a feast, to celebrate all the good realized by the combination of God's gifts and human labor. Contemplation too, if it wishes to be human, cannot remain a purely individual and interior activity; it must be expressed, shared with others through conversation, by celebration, and in the wider sense, by culture. The active repose of contemplation and community celebration can be an image of the life to come.

The Bible itself represents this life by images of activity: celebration of feasts, worship, the service of God, domination over the world. Even now, God's will is being done in heaven, and we pray that it may likewise be done on earth.[41] The servant who has been faithful in little things during this life, will not only enter into the joy of the Lord, but will be placed over many[42] and even over all His goods. That can be understood, in the first place, of the blessed who, before the Last Judgment, long to see their number completed. They regard us. Christ Himself is preparing a place for us; He does this while remaining with the Father and with us, in the Holy Spirit, but Himself nevertheless, all days even to the end of time. He intercedes for us, cares for us before the Father, as do the Saints. It is not only St. Theresa of Lisieux who spends her heaven doing good upon earth. The saints pray with us, not instead of us—we pray with them much more than we pray to them. This activity, with its touch of anxiety, labor and struggle, will cease at the moment of the definitive consummation, but celebration will remain.

---

[39] John 5, 17.
[40] Os. 2, 13; Is. 1, 13.
[41] Mt. 6, 10.
[42] Mt. 25, 21-23; Luke 19, 17 and 19.

If this sounds to us monotonous, it is because we need to rid ourselves of a neurotic over-esteem of productive work, and of a use not yet integrated and personalized of our "free time." But the deeper ground is an insufficient knowledge of God's power and life.

We have one last thing to say. In this systematization of the data of revelation, we have obviously stressed what is already good in our life, naturally and supernaturally. But our life does not consist entirely of good moments, there are also bad ones. It is not only the prelude to heaven, but the captivity of sin as well.[43] Therefore the consummation will also be full "deliverance."[44] The Father will not only make our joy full,[45] but He will remove all sadness: "Behold the tabernacle of God with men, and He will dwell with them. And they shall be His people, and God Himself with them shall be their God. And God shall wipe away all tears from their eyes, and death shall be no more. Nor mourning, nor crying, nor sorrow shall be any more; for the former things are passed away."[46]

[43]Luke 21, 28.
[44]Luke, *ibid.*
[45]John 15, 11.
[46]Apoc. 21, 3 ff.

INDEX OF NAMES

INDEX OF SUBJECT MATTER